AVIGNON OF THE POPES

Avignon of the Popes
City of Exiles

Edwin Mullins

SIGNAL BOOKS
Oxford

First published in 2007
This edition published in 2017 by
Signal Books Limited
36 Minster Road
Oxford
OX4 1LY
www.signalbooks.co.uk

This edition prepared for printing by Andrews UK Limited.

A catalogue record for this book is available from the British Library
ISBN 978-1-909930-58-2

Cover Images:
© Robert Weber/istockphoto; © Photos Daspet; © Fanelie Rosier/istockphoto;
© Catriona Davidson

Cover Design: Baseline Arts

Photos and illustrations:
© Rémy Cantin p.vii; © Catriona Davidson pp.ix, 20, 92, 142, 164, 169,
200, 226, 238, 240; © Photos Daspet pp.53 (Musée Pierre-de-Luxembourg de
Villeneuve-lès-Avignon), 107, 128, 237; © Edwin Mullins pp.24, 81, 127; ©
sassphoto/istockphoto p.14; © quesaquo/istockphoto p.42; © Jacques Mossot/
Nicolas Janberg ICS p.70; © Musée de Cluny p.108; © Manfred Konrad/istock p.
228; © Robert Weber/istockphoto p.230

Contents

Author's Preface

For part of each year I live and work in an area of Provence known as the Papal County—the *Comtat Venaissin*—even though no pope to my knowledge has set foot in the region for over six hundred years, and considerably more than two hundred years have elapsed since the Vatican exercised any authority over the county whatsoever. Yet traditions cling on. At eight o'clock every weekday morning close to our house a bus boldly decorated with a swipe of colour and bearing the legend "Cars Comtadin" takes on its cargo of village schoolchildren and proceeds to transport them in the direction of Carpentras, which is still the official capital of the papal Comtat.

Eleven miles beyond Carpentras stands Avignon, the former papal city, dominated by its hulk of a papal palace and ringed by massive ramparts which the popes erected in order to protect

themselves against eyes that were even greedier than theirs were.

In short, the popes themselves may have long departed, but their ghosts have not. Their images still gaze out at us haughtily from bare walls in the heart of the city.

Reminders of past glory: the seven Avignon popes and two anti-popes emblazoned on a wall in the rue Dorée in the centre of the city.

The story of this place and this region is one I have wanted to tell. The tale begins early in the fourteenth century when anarchy in Italy led to the capital of western Christianity being moved from Rome for the first and only time in history. It was a critical moment, and it resulted in seven successive popes remaining "in exile" for the next seventy years. The city chosen to replace Rome was Avignon. And depending on where you stood at the time they were seventy years of heaven, or of hell—opinions invariably ran to extremes, as did the behaviour of the popes themselves.

It was during this period of exile that the city witnessed some of the most turbulent events in the history of Christendom, among them the suppression of the Knights Templar and the last of the heretical Cathars, the first major onslaught of the plague (the Black Death), the final collapse of the crusading dream, and the first decades of the Hundred Years War between England and France, in which successive Avignon popes attempted to mediate. The papal flight from Rome was fiercely castigated by Dante in *The Divine Comedy*, while during the later years of exile in Avignon the enigmatic figure of Petrarch, the most celebrated poet and scholar of his day, loomed angrily over the city.

This is a portrait sketch of that era. And at the centre of the picture is Avignon itself, as it grew from being a relatively insignificant town on the River Rhône to become, albeit briefly, one of the great capitals of the world.

Île de la
Barthelasse

Rhône

Rhône

Pont
St.-Bénézet

St.-Nicolas

Boulevard de la Ligne

Boulevard St.-Lazare

Les
Pénitents
Noirs

Petit
Palais

Cathédrale
Nôtre-Dame-
des-Doms

Palais
des Papes

Rue Carreterie

Place des
Carmes

St.-Symphorien
des Carmes

University

Place de
l'Horloge

Rue Carnot

St.-Pierre

St.-Agricol

Place
Pignotte

La Visitation

Palais du
Roure

Musée
Calvet

Rue Thiers

Les
Halles

St.-Didier

Rue de la République

Rue Joseph Vernet

Bibliothèque
Ceccano

Chapelle des
Cordeliers

Rue des Teinturiers

Boulevard Raspail

St.-Martial

Rue St.-Michel

Boulevard St.-Michel

N

0   200
metres

AVIGNON

Avignon — the heart of the medieval city: cathedral and papal palace.

I

The Road from Rome

It was in August 1308 that Pope Clement V, a Frenchman, announced that the new home of the papacy was to be Avignon. And in the spring of the following year he moved there, to be joined soon afterwards by the papal court.

Avignon was then a small town perched on a sentinel rock overlooking the most southerly surviving bridge across the River Rhône and some fifty miles inland from the Mediterranean. Just as important as its strategic position was the fact that it was situated on the borders of the only territory owned by the papacy to lie safely outside Italy, and therefore beyond the reach of the political chaos which engulfed much of that land. Avignon also lay on the borders of France, whose monarch was the new pope's most powerful ally. All in all, Clement's choice seemed to make extremely good sense.

At that time Avignon had a population of scarcely more than five thousand inhabitants. Yet such was the impact of the papacy that within a few decades it came to grow larger than Rome itself and become one of the wealthiest and most glittering cities in Europe. To many who were drawn to Avignon from all over the known world it seemed a wonder of the world—not so much on account of its piety and godliness as for the overwhelming presence of Mammon: it was a city that dripped gold and jewels, a place of unmatched glamour and splendour. Hence to more severe observers the city was an object of loathing and contempt, a place where unholy opulence was coupled with greed, rapacity, nepotism, corruption, a shameless abuse of its power and wealth, and above all an outrageous moral laxity. In short Avignon seemed to be an abuse of everything that Christ had stood for.

Avignon is the city that was created during those golden, or rotten, years by seven successive popes. All of them were as different from each other as human nature could allow, though bound in a semblance of unity by the massive weight of their common role— the fact that they had been enthroned as the spiritual leaders of the Christian world. And it remains their city today, even though more than six hundred years have passed since their return to Rome in the year 1378. To stand on that sentinel rock is to stand on the shoulders of their history.

§

The first steps of the papal journey into exile were taken from another small hill-town several hundred miles further south, in southern Italy a short distance beyond Rome. This was Anagni. In the mid-thirteenth century Anagni was the birth-place of a certain Benedetto Gaetani (sometimes spelt Caetani), whose family were Roman nobility of considerable influence and power. As a young man Benedetto entered the church where he enjoyed a successful and by all accounts pious career, which culminated late in life in his election as pope in the year 1296, under the title Boniface VIII.

His period of office proved to be an ill-starred one. Diplomacy was never one of Boniface's natural assets. Wielding the arrogance of a Roman nobleman he managed to arouse the fury of the most autocratic monarch of the day, King Philip IV of France, known as Philip the Fair on account of his handsome bearing. The pontiff crossed swords with the French king principally by issuing two uncompromising papal bulls in rapid succession. Both had the same aim, to demonstrate the supremacy of the pope as God's representative on earth over any mere monarch. The first of these bulls placed all clergy and church property beyond the reach of grasping lay rulers by forbidding taxes being imposed on them without papal approval. The second bull, the famous *Unam Sanctum*, was even more challenging to Philip in its insistence that every human creature on this earth was subject to papal authority above any other.

To a monarch who held a vainglorious view of his own power and importance, as well as being perpetually short of cash, this was a double provocation in the extreme. Philip's reaction to what he saw as a piece of impertinent meddling by the papacy into temporal affairs was to burn the papal bulls publicly. He went further, pledging to have Boniface charged with heresy before a forthcoming general council of the church. Not to be outdone in the power stakes, Boniface reacted with characteristic lack of compromise by preparing to issue a further bull against the French king—this time one of excommunication. This was any pope's ultimate weapon. He might lack the worldly might of kings and emperors, but in a society which never questioned God's supreme authority over the affairs of mankind a pope was perceived as having the ear of the Almighty and therefore the right to pronounce the judgment of heaven on mortal beings here on earth, however lofty and powerful they might be. Even kings would quail. Unless they received absolution excommunication meant that they could never be received into the company of other Christians. They could receive no rites or sacraments of the church. They would be permitted no Christian burial when they died. And— a prospect to chill the heart of the proudest monarch—they would go to hell. For the most humble believer such punishment would be hard to bear. For a monarch accustomed to command all around him the blow could be catastrophic. He became an outlaw in the very world he ruled.

Unfortunately for Boniface there was another, more sinister, enemy closer to hand than the French king. Among the numerous rivalries that were forever erupting into violence between Roman noblemen, one of the most vicious was the rift between the Gaetani family, to whom the pope belonged, and the equally arrogant Colonna family. The core of the dispute was over certain lands in the Roman *campagna* which had long been claimed by both parties; but more recently matters had grown much uglier than a mere argument over grazing rights. The feud had developed into charges of homicide.

In essence what occurred was this. At the time of Boniface's election the papal Curia, the pope's administrative body, included two Colonna cardinals. Their dislike of the new pope derived from the long-standing feud between the two Roman families. But with the election of a Gaetani pope his enemies felt the need to bring matters to a head. They needed a *cause célèbre*: and this the two Colonna cardinals found in the somewhat murky circumstances that had surrounded the death of Boniface's immediate predecessor, Celestine V (later to be canonized). Celestine had been an elderly monk who soon came to feel the office of pontiff to be too heavy a burden, and pleaded to be allowed to resign and return to his monastery. There arose considerable opposition to this request on the grounds that popes were elected by the will of God acting through the mere agency of the cardinals, and therefore had no right to abdicate. The man who persuaded his fellow-cardinals to accept such an unprecedented state of affairs and allow Celestine to resign was none other than Benedetto Gaetani. Furthermore in a very short time it was Benedetto who found himself elected in Celestine's place. Within two years Celestine was dead, having spent his last days not in a monk's cell as he had requested, but immured in a castle where his successor had felt it advisable to keep him, for reasons which were never explained.

There was never any proof of bribery or foul play on Cardinal Gaetani's part. None the less the circumstances surrounding the new pope's swift ascent to the papal throne, and his subsequent behaviour towards the aged Celestine, were sufficiently dubious to provide ammunition for his enemies. Accordingly the two Colonna cardinals dramatically raised the temperature of the dispute by openly accusing Boniface of being his predecessor's murderer.

Having levelled this sensational charge against the pontiff they added further fuel to the blaze by seizing a large quantity of papal treasure. At this point Boniface, never a man of moderation, retaliated with equal belligerence: he recruited an armed militia which proceeded to attack and demolish a number of Colonna castles in the area around Rome, so enabling the pope to distribute their lands among members of his own family, the Gaetani.

The family feud had now become open war. In a hasty act of self-protection the two Colonna cardinals took flight, seeking refuge in the company of the king of France, Philip the Fair, Boniface's sworn enemy.

The next chapter in this sordid tale has a predictable ring considering the vindictive nature of all those concerned, and the combustible state of affairs that had been created between them. A new character now steps on the stage, one who is to play a major part in the drama. He was a French lawyer by the name of Guillaume de Nogaret, who was one of Philip the Fair's most trusted ministers with the official title of Keeper of the Seals. In effect he was the king's right-hand man and trouble-shooter.

This was a moment in French history when lawyers were beginning to represent a new race of influential advisers to rulers and churchmen alike. Knowledge of civil law and particularly canon law was becoming an invaluable tool in stabilizing a ruler's finances as well as in the exercise of political power generally. A little legal alchemy could do wonders for an indigent ruler. (It is no accident that all seven churchmen who were to become Avignon popes had previously been successful lawyers, or at least had received a rigorous legal training.) As a clever and cool-headed adviser Nogaret was particularly useful to Philip the Fair: and it was he who had been given the task of preparing the charges which the king was determined to bring against Pope Boniface at the forthcoming general council of the church.

There was one extra, and strictly personal, reason why Nogaret may have relished formulating charges against a supreme pontiff. Nogaret was a Gascon, from the Toulouse district, which less than a century earlier had been an area that was predominantly Cathar in faith—in other words adherents to that heretical sect which had been so ruthlessly suppressed by order of the papacy (about which more later). In fact Nogaret's own Cathar grandfather had been burnt at the stake as a condemned heretic. Such family history might well have ignited a hatred of Rome in Nogaret's heart, and brought him delight at the opportunity for revenge.

In the event what happened next was more extreme than either Philip the Fair or Guillaume de Nogaret could have anticipated, or even wished. The French king felt the need to act swiftly, knowing that Boniface was preparing to excommunicate him, and was determined to make the first move. Accordingly, in September 1303, he sent Nogaret to Italy in order to test the mood of the pontiff and alert him to the fact that Philip was bringing severe charges against him in the council of the church. But other activities were already under way. Whether by accident or design (it has never been entirely clear which), Nogaret found himself in the company of an armed rabble which had been assembled by members of the Colonna family including the two self-exiled cardinals. With or without Nogaret's consent, and with or without the knowledge of the French king (again we do not know), the mob was bent on abducting Pope Boniface and forcibly removing him to France where he was to stand trial on charges not only of heresy, but also of sodomy and the murder of his predecessor.

The pope was not in Rome at the time, but staying in the Gaetani family palace at Anagni, between Rome and Naples. On 7 September the Colonna mob burst into the palace. In what has become known as "the Outrage of Anagni" they seized and bound the horrified Boniface, then led him away on horseback, humiliatingly—it has been claimed—set facing the rear of the horse in a manner commonly reserved for thieves and petty criminals. Further insults seem to have been heaped on the elderly pontiff in captivity: he may even have been roughed up by his Colonna guards. A few days later the people of Anagni, incensed by such treatment of their pope, who was also their local lord, forced their way into the prison where he was being held, and rescued him.

Within six weeks, however, Boniface was dead. Whether his death was a direct result of the ill-treatment he had received, or whether it was shock, or perhaps a heart attack or a stroke, has never been established. But clearly he was a broken old man. Maybe the most crippling blow of all had been the harsh reminder that God's representative on earth was, like the very first Bishop of Rome, St. Peter, and indeed Jesus himself, vulnerable to the actions of a brutish world.

One thing is certain: the legacy of the shocking fate of Boniface was to instil in the minds of his successors an acute sense of insecurity. Popes could no longer consider themselves safe just because they were popes: any notion of their invulnerability had been buried with Boniface. Fear of a repetition of the Anagni outrage was to have a profound influence on papal policy in the decades to follow, and particularly on relations with the monarch who was widely seen as having been the prime instigator of the Anagni kidnapping, Philip the Fair of France.

§

The immediate effect of the events at Anagni was a conviction among the cardinals that the headquarters of the Christian empire could no longer be safely entrusted to an anarchic city like Rome, or even indeed to Italy as a whole. It was time to flee.

At first the flight was not very far. The new pope, Benedict XI, was another Italian: he had been the Cardinal Archbishop of Ostia, the port of Rome, and so was all too well acquainted with the turbulence prevailing in the papal city and in the surrounding *campagna*. Accordingly he chose to move the papal court further north, to Perugia. The city was not at this stage a papal possession: none the less in the interminable power struggle between supporters of the pope and those of the Holy Roman Emperor Perugia had long been firmly on the side of the papacy. It was relatively stable, and relatively safe.

But Benedict never actually made it to Perugia. He died on the way in July 1304, having held office for less than a year. The cardinals were now in even greater disarray. They found themselves obliged to foregather in Perugia, where few of them wished to be—least of all the French cardinals who would have preferred not to be in Italy at all. Even though the papacy owned no fewer than seven areas of Italy outside Rome, it was already clear that not one of these papal states was politically stable enough for the papacy to be moved there permanently. In fact many of them were no longer even controlled by the papal authorities, but had been seized and plundered by a variety of opportunist warlords.

Not surprisingly the cardinals themselves were in hopeless disagreement over who should be chosen as the next pope. Having two pontiffs die within a single year was hardly propitious. The Italian cardinals were ever-more-deeply divided among themselves, their differences exacerbated by relentless family feuds and nepotistic interests. The political condition of the Italian peninsula, and of Rome in particular, further contributed to the unlikelihood of a consensus ever being reached. There was increasing outside pressure too, above all from the formidable monarch who had already caused so much mischief in papal affairs, King Philip the Fair of France. The longer the stalemate in Perugia continued the stronger the French king's influence on the electoral process grew, even from a distance; until after eleven months had passed, and still no new pope had been elected, there seemed to be only one course of action about which there was general agreement—that a successor must be sought from outside the college of cardinals.

This was the opportunity the French king had been waiting for. Philip had a candidate in mind, one he felt sure the exhausted cardinals would gratefully accept. The man he favoured was a Frenchman, therefore quite uninvolved in the petty rivalries so dominant in Italy, and in consequence unlikely to ruffle any feathers among the Italian cardinals. Naturally he would be welcomed by the French cardinals; and of course, being Philip's appointee, there would be no question of any challenge to the absolute authority of the monarch in the manner so imperiously handed out by the late Pope Boniface. In other words the new pope would be in the French king's pocket.

Philip got his way. On 5 June 1305 ten out of the fifteen cardinals who made up the Sacred College in Perugia voted for a man who was not even a cardinal but a distinguished canon lawyer from Aquitaine who was also Archbishop of Bordeaux and—when he heard the news of his election—was an extremely surprised man indeed.

He was Bertrand de Got. And as Clement V he was soon to become the first of the seven Avignon popes.

§

Clement V has been treated roughly by historians, owing largely to his inconsistent and often treacherous contribution towards the suppression of the Knights Templar (about which more in the next chapter). He has been seen, with some justice, as a weak and vacillating man who invariably acceded to the demands of the French king as soon as any pressure was put upon him, which Philip was ruthless at doing. He may even be said to have got the Avignon papacy off to a thoroughly bad start. For all nine years of his papacy Clement was a man forever caught between a desire to follow the right and honourable path (such as establishing peace between France and England, thereby releasing funds for yet another crusade) and fear of a French king who had already been instrumental in destroying one pope, and might not hesitate to destroy another if needs be.

Clement was by nature a peacemaker who forever found himself compelled to deal with men of violence. This conflict of outlooks was further complicated by the fact that as a Gascon his native region of Aquitaine was under English rule, while as a Frenchman he remained a subject of the king of France. To this conflict of loyalties was added a further burden. Clement was a sick man: for his entire period in office he was slowly dying of what is believed to have been a form of stomach cancer. For all these reasons Clement deserves our sympathy and concern, though perhaps not too much of it. The nine years of his papacy offer a sad demonstration that even being the delegate of the Almighty may be insufficient to shore up an essentially weak man in the face of ruthless earthly power.

At the outset he seems to have been confident that, even in the face of this earthly power, he would still be able to shape the course of history. When the news of his election reached him he was in the town of Lusignan, near Poitiers. Clement immediately returned to his archbishopric, Bordeaux, where he made a public vow—to broker a peace treaty between France and England and, once this had been achieved, to return the papacy to Rome.

These inaugural vows illuminate the first of Clement's failures. Had he succeeded in his twin ambitions history could have taken two very different paths: there might have been no Hundred Years War between England and France, and there would certainly have been no Avignon of the popes. In addition, historians might have been a good deal kinder to him. Clement's next vow—also never achieved—was to be crowned in the city of Vienne, in the Dauphiné province, which was not at that time within the borders of France but part of the Holy Roman Empire. His choice was sensible enough: from the outset he resolved to set his new role as pope at a certain distance from the monarch to whom he owed his election. He did not wish to be seen as a puppet of the French king, which many among the cardinals, especially the Italians, already perceived him to be.

Clement's reign was destined to be blighted by forlorn hopes. Even the place of his coronation came to be decided by the man who had made him pope in the first place. Philip the Fair was not a man prepared to see his protégé crowned in another ruler's territory. It is never clear precisely what kind of pressure the French king chose to bring to bear whenever he needed Clement to change his mind: but pressure there certainly was on this occasion, as on many another, and it is reasonable to assume that the threat of physical force was never far away: certainly an armed militia was invariably close at hand whenever the two men met. Clement would also have been all too well aware that only two years had passed since the abduction and death of Pope Boniface at Anagni. History could easily repeat itself.

Philip's will prevailed, as usual. The coronation took place on 1 November at Lyon in the church of St.-Just, significantly in that area of the city on the west bank of the River Saône, which lay in France, unlike the area on the east bank, which was part of the Holy Roman Empire.

The king was present in person, the ceremony being followed at his insistence by a sumptuous procession through the streets of the city, which he made sure was as much a demonstration of French royal pomp and power as a celebration of Clement's ascent to the highest office in Christendom. What the ceremony conveyed would have been clear to all who were present: that there was now a French pope, and hereafter the papacy would belong unequivocally to France.

There was one hitch in the proceedings: at the height of the procession a wall on which onlookers had scrambled to gawp at the passing dignitaries in their finery collapsed, killing a number of people including a member of the king's entourage, the Duke of Brittany, and causing the horse of the newly-crowned pope to shy. The pope himself was thrown to the ground, and his papal tiara sent rolling away in the dirt. A large ruby that had been set in it promptly vanished, never to be seen again.

Whether or not the accident struck those present as an ill omen, no one would have been in the least surprised if the papal ruby had ended up decorating the French royal crown. What is certainly true is that the image of papal authority scrabbling in the dust at the feet of the French king mercilessly illustrates history's judgment on this unfortunate pope.

Clement was already a sick man, and events in Lyon cannot have helped his physical condition. Immediately after his coronation he retreated first to Vienne, where the papal court was temporarily encamped. From here he journeyed for a brief period of rest to the great Benedictine abbey of Cluny, and finally returned to Bordeaux, the seat of his former archbishopric. Here his health seems to have worsened further, and he remained in the Bordeaux region for the whole of the following year while the papal court continued its nomadic existence, establishing itself eventually at Poitiers where Clement himself took up residence in the spring of 1307. Here he had a further meeting with the French king, discussing among other things the fate of the Knights Templar, shortly to be arrested en masse—against Clement's will. But as ever the pope's wishes counted for little when opposed by those of Philip the Fair.

It may be that so many sharp differences which had by now opened up between himself and King Philip, together with his own ineffectiveness in standing up to the monarch who considered him his puppet, were what drove Clement finally to seek a papal residence that lay beyond the borders of France, and therefore free of Philip's direct authority. In the event, in August the following year, 1308, Clement announced that the papal court would shortly be leaving Poitiers, and that its new "home" was to be Avignon.

It was a shrewd decision. The boundary of France at that time was the River Rhône, and Avignon lay on the farther bank. So, setting up the papal seat there would give some measure of assurance to the sceptics that the new pope was not intending to be merely the French king's factotum. The river would act as something of a safety barrier against the bullying monarch just across the water. At the same time the city, with its all-important bridge across the Rhône, the Pont St.-Bénézet, was strategically placed as a link between France to the west and those countries to the east, Italy and the Holy Roman Empire in particular. All popes needed lines of communication that were open to the outside world, and here the Rhône supplied a vital connection between the nations of northern Europe and those abutting the Mediterranean. Avignon was a hinge linking two areas of the continent. What was more, should the papacy shortly return to Rome, as Pope Clement intended, certainly at first, then the great port of Marseille was close at hand.

A further point of advantage was that Avignon was owned by a French nobleman, Charles II of Anjou, who was the king's uncle. Charles boasted the grandiose titles of Count of Provence, King of Naples, King of the Two Sicilies and King of Jerusalem, yet in accordance with the complex social system still pertaining in feudal Europe he was also, by tradition, a vassal of the papacy. Effectively this meant that, while retaining ownership of the city, Charles was legally bound to extend personal loyalties to the pope as his overlord. In other words Clement could count on a friend and supporter, even if that friend happened to be the king's uncle.

§

By the time Clement chose to settle here Avignon had known better days. It had enjoyed a long and varied history. Stone Age man had settled round its now-celebrated rock. About the time of Christ members of a Celtic tribe knew the place as Auoention, which translates as "Lord of the Waters". The Romans, when they colonized the entire area as their "Province of Rome" (i.e. Provence), adapted the Celtic name into the Latin Avenio, or Aventius. It soon became a flourishing Roman city with its forum, or marketplace, occupying what is now the central square of modern Avignon, the Place de l'Horloge. Fragments of that Roman forum still survive, piled up unceremoniously on the edge of the Rue St.-Etienne.

After the collapse of the Roman Empire waves of barbarian invasions struck the city between the fifth and eighth centuries: Saracens, Franks, Burgundians, Ostrogoths, Franks again, Saracens again, the final insult being delivered by Charlemagne's bellicose grandfather, Charles Martel, who in the course of driving out the

Saracens in the mid-eighth century managed to destroy the city and slaughter its inhabitants not just once, but twice. Place-names inevitably endure longer than memories; in the heart of what would have been the medieval city runs a small street, the Rue Rouge, which still commemorates that orgy of bloodshed.

With the Saracen menace finally over by the eleventh century Avignon began at last to enjoy a period of wealth and prosperity as a semi-independent state. Its key position in the Rhône valley made it a natural trading corridor between the Mediterranean and northern Europe. The present cathedral was begun, Nôtre-Dame des Doms (its name deriving from the Latin *domus* denoting the "place of the bishop"), and in the twelfth century protective walls fringed by a moat were constructed encircling the entire city. There were by now no fewer than three small harbours along the stretch of the river below the great rock, the principal one being next to Avignon's new masterpiece of engineering, the bridge of St.-Bénézet which linked the city to France across the River Rhône. It was one thousand yards in length, eight years under construction and the last bridge

across the river before the Mediterranean. Originally the Pont St.-Bénézet consisted of no fewer than twenty-two arches, all but four of which were swept away by flood-waters in the seventeenth century. What remained was the irresistible legend of people dancing "tous en rond"—which actually took place almost certainly "*sous* le pont d'Avignon" rather than "*sur* le pont", most likely on the small green Barthelasse Island in the Rhône over which the wondrous bridge once crossed.

Then darkness fell. Early in the thirteenth century Avignon became the victim of an accident of feudal loyalties. The city found itself on the losing side of one of the most bloodthirsty ideological struggles of the entire Middle Ages—the cynical and inglorious "crusade" launched by the papacy and the French king against the heretical sect in the south known as the Cathars. Avignon suffered appalling reprisals as a direct result of that campaign simply because the city and much of the surrounding area were at that time ceded to the Counts of Toulouse, who were traditionally supporters of the Cathars.

Their story has often been told, and only the briefest outline is appropriate here. The Cathars were far and away the most popular heretical sect within Christianity before the Reformation three centuries later, and in many respects they were the natural precursors of the Protestants, "protesting" as they did against the venality and corruption of the established church of the day (the name Cathar most likely deriving from the Greek *katharos*, meaning "pure"). The Cathars, or Cathari, flourished particularly strongly in the Languedoc region of southern France, where by the end of the twelfth century they had largely come to replace orthodox Catholicism, with their own administrative organization, their own bishops, their own doctrines and religious services.

The core of the Cathar faith was a startlingly simple one: it was a belief that the world was not created by God alone, but by God and the Devil, God having been responsible for all matters of the spirit, and the Devil for the material world. In consequence the human body together with all its physical functions was held by the Cathari to be evil, and only the human spirit contained within that body was considered good. Hence the only people free of the stain of Satan were those who renounced all pleasures of the flesh including, naturally, sexual intercourse. These Cathari elite were known as *perfecti*, or "perfects", and they were seen as the saviours of mankind on this earth, presiding over the rest of the human race, not as priests or moral tyrants, but benevolently, as men who led their chosen ascetic life humbly within the community they served. The effect of this benevolent presence—perverse though it may seem—was to permit ordinary people to get on with their own sinful lives unburdened by guilt, confident in the knowledge that none of it was their fault, and without having to endure the tyranny of the weekly sermon and the weekly confession which the Catholic Church imposed upon them. And to make their daily existence even more comfortable the Cathar faith offered to those approaching the end of their lives a formal ceremony of moral reprieve called the *consolamentum*, allowing them to be reclaimed by God at the last gasp so to speak, thereby enabling a lifetime spent in the clutches of the Devil to be wiped away at a stroke.

Not surprisingly, so pragmatic a solution to the Christian obsession with sin contributed greatly to the widespread popularity of the Cathar faith. And it is hard to see at first glance why so benign and peace-loving a doctrine should have come to be represented as a diabolical threat to the orthodox church.

In fact, until towards the end of the twelfth century there seems to have been little serious attempt by the church authorities to suppress the Cathars, or even to censure them. But in a very short time the mood changed. In the year 1187 Jerusalem fell to the Saracens. It is impossible to overestimate the force of that blow to the leaders of Christendom: the fact that the most holy of all cities had fallen to the Infidel was a traumatic reversal. The crusading movement upon which so many Christian hopes had been pinned for more than a century was facing defeat. Islam was once again in the ascendant.

And as fears of the enemy without spread, so fears of the enemy within were rekindled. Tolerance became seen as a sign of weakness, and orthodoxy became the raft to which Christian leaders clung. Heresy was the new evil, to be plucked out.

In this new mood of vigilance events moved swiftly against the Cathars. Pope Innocent III sent an envoy to the Count of Toulouse, Raymond VI, in a bid to persuade him to act against the heretics. Instead, in 1208 the papal envoy was murdered, and Count Raymond was widely held responsible for the crime, directly or indirectly. An army led by the Cistercian Abbot of Cîteaux, supported by barons from northern France keen to seize whatever they could, descended on Languedoc and plundered the region, The entire population of Béziers (seven thousand people at least) was put to the sword, Catholic and Cathar alike, the godly abbot having proclaimed "Kill them all, for the Lord knows which are His."

This was only the beginning. Six years later, in 1215, the pope convoked the Fourth Lateran Council in which the orthodox dogma of the Catholic Church was precisely spelt out, no longer allowing room for variants of any kind. The outcome of this historic gathering was the birth within twelve years of that most celebrated instrument of repression in the history of Christianity, the Inquisition. From now onwards the Cathars were political and moral outlaws. Count Raymond's son and successor, Raymond VII, continued to hold out against what he saw (accurately enough) as land-grabbling adventurers from northern France. In 1226 Avignon, under his charge, defiantly closed its gates and refused passage to the army of the French king, Louis VIII. A three-month siege followed until finally the inhabitants were starved into submission. The king seized the city. Count Raymond himself was compelled to be stripped to the waist and whipped at the altar of Avignon's cathedral with a rope round his neck. The city itself was ransacked and much of it destroyed, including its encircling ramparts.

As for Count Raymond, he was now deprived of all his lands. In 1229 the French king imposed the Treaty of Paris on the hapless count, who was forced to relinquish Languedoc as well as the county of Provence. Both were absorbed into the kingdom of France, a transfer of ownership which effectively marked the end of the independence of much of the entire south for ever. It is an arresting thought that had it not been for the "crusade" against the Cathars this whole region might never have become part of France.

Seventeen years later the next French King Louis IX (St. Louis as he became) handed Provence, along with Avignon, to his brother Charles, Count of Anjou. Finally, in 1274, by agreement with the count, the territory of Provence was divided into two: the area south of the River Durance, but including Avignon which lay just to the north, remained in the possession of the counts of Anjou, while the rest of the area north of the river was ceded to the papacy to become the Vatican's sole possession outside Italy. This was seen as a just reward for the assistance the popes had given to the suppression of the Cathars, and for the enormous gains of territory which had fallen to the French crown as a direct result.

This northern area of Provence accordingly became the "papal county", known (as it still is today) as the Comtat Venaissin, so-named after the small hill-town of Venasque which had been the seat of the local bishopric from as early as the sixth century.

§

There is no eye-witness account of the historic occasion when Pope Clement V and the papal court finally reached Avignon in the spring of the year 1309. One imagines the arrival would have been by river, southwards down the Rhône valley, docking at the principal quay which lay just below the towering Rocher des Doms and close to the Pont St.-Bénézet, still spanning the full width of the Rhône with its impressive stretch of twenty-two arches.

Yet at this stage the grand arrival was seen as only temporary: Clement was still planning to fulfil his vow to return the papacy to Rome in the not-too-distant future. Avignon was seen as a mere stepping-stone (though not for very long: continued political upheaval in Italy soon forced him to postpone indefinitely his plan to move on).

The city when he entered it was a medieval labyrinth still struggling to recover from the French king's savage onslaught almost a century earlier. For churchmen accustomed to many of the finer comforts of life—however nomadic they had been compelled to be for the past four years—their new residence was to prove far from ideal: very few of those habitual comforts were available in Avignon. Both the pope and the papal court had no choice but to make the best of it. In a city of only a few thousand inhabitants accommodation was hard to come by. Clement and his immediate staff of servants and secretaries took up residence at a Dominican priory in the western part of the city, while his wider entourage settled wherever they were able to find a roof.

Pope Clement was a chronically sick man by the time he reached Avignon, and the prevailing conditions of the city were profoundly unsuited to his needs. Not surprisingly it was the Comtat which was to become his haven of rest for the five years of life that remained to him. Unfortunately the world stage would not often allow him any such privilege. Clement was not a man who should ever have been called upon to play high politics, and like many others who have been thrust into a demanding public role by some freak of history his reaction to those demands was to make decisions which were often impulsive and fatally inconsistent. Clement became a victim of a role which he had never chosen, and to which he was never suited. As it transpired, those last five years of his life were to be among the most tortuous in the entire history of the papacy.

The still surviving papal vineyard looks over the Pont St.-Bénézet, which once linked Avignon to France over the Rhône, while the Tour Philippe-le-Bel kept a threatening watch on the papal city.

2

Fallen Temples

After so many years of wandering it is ironical that Clement discovered little joy in the place where he finally chose to settle. He found himself in a city with virtually no protective walls, streets that were muddy and narrow, with threads of waterways that were stinking and foul, and buildings for the most part mean and run-down. Altogether it was a thoroughly unsavoury place, and in high summer insufferably hot. Through sheer lack of space business meetings were sometimes held in cemeteries, which were themselves so overcrowded that graves were dug too shallow and pigs were to be found digging up the recently dead. One ambassador from Aragon was so appalled by the filth and stench of the narrow streets that he became ill and was compelled to return home.

Besides, the pope himself was ill too. The bouts of intense stomach pain he suffered were becoming more frequent, and increasingly he tried whenever possible to live a life of seclusion. The Dominican convent where he had his private quarters was never private enough, and Clement took to spending as much time as he could in the relative tranquillity of the papal county to the east of Avignon, the Comtat Venaissin. Here, among the mountains and river-valleys where the air was sweet and he could be reminded of his beloved Gascony, he was sometimes able to find a measure of calm and live the life of a recluse, which his state of health as well as his nature yearned for.

In Clement's day, as now, the central area of the Comtat was a fertile plain watered by streams from the mountains and walled in

Comtat Venaissin

N

0   5
km

Valréas

River Rhône

River Aigues

River Ouvèze

Vaison

M o n t
V e n t o u x

Malaucène

Orange

Châteauneuf
-du-Pape

Mormoiron

Carpentras

Roquemaure

Monteux

Sorgues

Venasque

Pernes

Villeneuve

Fontaine-de
Vaucluse

River Rhône

Avignon

L'Isle-sur-Sorgue

River Durance

Châteaurenard

FRANCE

*Comtat
Venaissin*

Cavaillon

on three sides by scrubby hills and high plateaux slashed by sudden gorges. All around lay plentiful evidence of the county's feudal past and bloodstained history dating back to the dark centuries when Saracens and other foreign invaders regularly plundered this land. Like the rest of Provence the region had always been a vulnerable middle-ground for marauding armies in whatever direction they were eventually heading, east or west, north or south, or sweeping inland from the shores of the Mediterranean.

The lay-out of the towns and small settlements of the Comtat offers proof to this day of those embattled centuries—either perched on hilltops or encircled by formidable walls. The small town of Venasque, which gave the papal county its name, became the seat of the local bishop from as early as the sixth century by virtue of its relatively secure position on a steep hill overlooking the open plain to the north and backed by the wild Vaucluse plateau to the south. The sixth-century baptistery and eleventh-century church still stand, and so does part of the massive fortress guarding the town, with its Tour Sarrasines and its walls ten feet thick.

Closer to Avignon, down in the plain, is the riverside town of Pernes (now Pernes-les-Fontaines), which in Pope Clement's day was the capital and administrative centre of the Comtat. The huge fortified walls, many of which survive, originally protected the castle of the Counts of Toulouse, the dynasty which owned this region as well as much of the rest of Provence until as supporters of the heretical Cathars they were deprived of their lands by the French king, and Count Raymond VII of Toulouse (as described in Chapter One) was stripped to the waist and whipped at the altar of Avignon cathedral.

Pope Clement may well have stayed in Pernes, but a more favourite retreat during his prolonged bouts of illness lay a few miles to the north-west, at Monteux, where one of his nephews had bought the local castle. One single tower of it remains, half-buried in the centre of the modern town, a massive squat edifice proudly described on a nearby plaque as "La Tour Clémentine".

In the sweltering summer months the pope preferred to retreat to the mountains. Towards the northern borders of the Comtat rises Mont Ventoux, at more than six thousand feet the highest mountain in Provence and the focus of a great deal of myth and magic. On the north side a dramatic gush of water bursts from the base of the mountain. A short distance away, set back from the road to Malaucène, stands the modest eleventh-century chapel of Nôtre-Dame-du-Groseau, its name deriving from Groselos, the Celtic god of springs. An unprepossessing little box of a building, it is easy to pass by without noticing it, and permission has to be sought at Malaucène to go inside: but there on the dimly-lit limestone walls and Romanesque arches are ghostly traces of early-medieval paintings, and in one place, barely visible, the painted escutcheon of Pope Clement V. The chapel is all that remains of a Benedictine priory which was

Clement's favourite retreat from the summer oven of the city, and records quoted inside the chapel make it clear that the pope spent more than four hundred days at Groseau over the course of the five summers of his Avignon papacy—an average of almost three months each year. Several papal bulls issued during this period are inscribed "du Grosel, près Malaucène".

Not that Avignon itself was entirely without its consolations. In the heart of

the city, on a high terrace backing on to the cathedral and overlooking the famous bridge, is a plot of land which points to a trait in Clement's nature that feels unexpected in a man of his temperament and style of living. It is an immaculate vineyard. In fact Clement, like most of his successors at Avignon, was a lover of good wine. As Archbishop of Bordeaux he had been given an estate by his brother a short distance from the city, at Pessac, and which he planted with vines in the year 1300. The estate later came to produce some of the finest Bordeaux wines, mostly exported to England since this was part of English-owned Aquitaine. (The estate still produces a Grand Cru wine under the name Château Pape Clément.)

On arrival in Avignon Clement soon set about planting vines nearby. It was not at that time a notable vine-growing area, and most quality wines were shipped downriver from Burgundy where the Cistercians had established a successful wine industry around Beaune on what was then monastery land. The site Clement chose was a stony windswept ridge overlooking the Rhône Valley a few miles north of the city. Clearly the knowledge of viniculture he had acquired in Bordeaux stood him in good stead because the site was soon to produce wine that was even more celebrated than his previous vineyard near Bordeaux had yielded. The place had as yet no resounding name: it was merely a vineyard on a hill. That was to wait for the Clement's immediate successor, John XXII, a man who appreciated his wine so enthusiastically that he built an extensive castle amid the vineyards on that stony ridge so that he could imbibe there whenever he chose. The place became known as Châteauneuf-du-Pape.

§

Much of the Avignon Pope Clement would have known has long since been swept away. But just a few of the grander buildings from that dark era have survived; and one of these, now privately-owned, is hidden away behind locked doors at the far end of an unprepossessing *cul de sac* in the heart of the old city. Time has not treated it well. All that is visible from the outside is a walled-up Gothic window next to a massive stone buttress, and to the right of the buttress what must once have been an elegant carved portal, now savagely decapitated leaving only the ghostly imprint of a pointed arch which once surmounted it. Hidden beyond those doors are further unexpected hints of past splendour: a lofty cavern of a room which is handsomely rib-vaulted, the arches crossing overhead like slender branches and rising from slim pilasters set into the walls on either side.

The building was once the private chapel of the Knights Templar, built in the thirteenth century and originally a part of their local *commanderie*, or headquarters, here in Avignon. The grim condition of the chapel is symbolic of the Templars' own fate. The story of their destruction is a sordid one which does no credit whatsoever to the two chief protagonists in that black drama, King Philip the Fair of France and the man he had promoted as pope, Clement V.

There are many roots to the story of the Templars' downfall, some of them inextricably entangled; yet two of them seem more prominent than any others. They are the enormous wealth of the Knights on the one hand, and the French king's equally enormous lack of funds on the other. Whatever other factors may have contributed to their downfall, without these two conditions the Templars would certainly have survived—at least for a time. As it is they were destined to be sacrificed on the altar of royal greed. One pertinent question, to which there can be no clear answer, is: might they still have survived had Pope Clement felt able to resist Philip's incessant bullying and clung to his initial refusal to condemn them as heretics?

The long drama of the Templars began in Jerusalem almost two centuries before, early in the twelfth century and a few decades after the First Crusade, at a time when the Christian armies were holding a tenuous grip on the Holy Land. It was then that a band of crusader knights from Burgundy and the Champagne district of France were awarded a wing of the royal palace in Jerusalem by the Christian king of the city, Baldwin II, the palace itself occupying the site of Solomon's temple as described in the Bible. The purpose of these French crusaders was to establish a religious order of knighthood dedicated to the protection of the holy places in Palestine, as well as to the safety of pilgrims who had begun to arrive in the Holy Land in considerable numbers. The community they formed was therefore essentially military in function, but it was run on monastic lines. They called themselves the "Poor Knights of Christ and of the Temple of Solomon", and each knight was required to take vows of chastity and (ironically in view of the order's future wealth) of poverty.

A short while later their rule of life came to be written down by that passionate ascetic St. Bernard of Clairvaux. And like the Cistercian Order for which Bernard was also largely responsible, the Templars began to prosper mightily. Their numbers increased to an estimated 20,000 until they became in effect the guardians of the Crusader Kingdom in Palestine. They garrisoned every fort and every town of any size, and in the course of their operations they gained an awesome reputation for deeds of valour. They became the most feared army of their day, and the acknowledged champions of Christendom. In consequence gifts of castles and large estates began to be showered upon them from grateful rulers and noblemen in France, Spain and England, until by the middle of the twelfth century they had come to own extensive property right across the continent of Europe.

This combination of armed strength and vast landed wealth led unerringly to a further role for the knights: they became unrivalled in being able to transport money and precious goods safely from one city or country to another—a priceless asset in an unstable world. As a result they rapidly became bankers, earning a reputation even higher than that of the Jews for financial acumen.

They soon came to manage the finances of monarchs, including (again ironically in view of their future fate) the kings of France. Their temple in Paris was in everything but name the world's bank. This was the pinnacle of their power.

Inevitably such a degree of affluence aroused jealousy. So long as the Templars' military prowess in securing the Crusader Kingdom was unquestioned those antagonisms remained for the most part beneath the surface. But once the Christian hold on the Bible lands began to weaken under the impact of the resurgent armies of Islam opposition began to mount. Jerusalem itself fell to the might of Saladin in 1187, fewer than seventy years after the foundation of the Templars' Order. And though the Crusader Kingdom continued to hang on for more than another century it was always a losing battle, with city after city gradually falling into the hands of the Muslims.

Finally, in the year 1291, the last Christian stronghold was overrun—the port of Acre, in what is now northern Israel. The Templars' battles were effectively over for good, and the knights retreated across the eastern Mediterranean to Cyprus where they set up their new headquarters.

With the ending of their military role their principal *raison d'être* had come to an end too. What remained was their wealth and the power and influence that went with it. They were now bankers and landlords, not soldiers. At the same time, having once been proud symbols of the crusading era, they found themselves cast as its scapegoat: they now took much of the blame for an ashamed and disgraced Christendom. Instead of being heroes they were seen as villains, or at least as parasites, profiteers, a body of men engaged in little beyond feathering their own nests.

It is not clear at what precise moment King Philip the Fair of France set his sights on pulling the Templars down. Tradition relates that there had been no apparent disagreement between the monarch and the people who were effectively his bankers.

Relations seem to have been perfectly cordial: in fact during Philip's bitter quarrel with Pope Boniface VIII (as related in the previous chapter) the Templars had openly supported the French king, even though the Order was in fact subject to the direct authority of the papacy. Nothing in what we can see of their relationship at that time suggests anything other than harmony and mutual self-interest. The Templars looked after the king's money, and in return they received the support of the most influential monarch in Europe.

Unfortunately the king's money was evaporating rapidly. This was due not to any incompetence on the part of the Templars as bankers, but to long-drawn-out military campaigns which the king was waging in Flanders; added to which large areas of land in France, namely Aquitaine, were the property of the kings of England. Accordingly all revenues from those territories, instead of swelling the royal coffers in Paris, were now crossing the Channel. Philip had already resorted to the desperate measure of debasing the currency, but this was only a temporary solution, and it was nowhere near enough.

Philip's radical change of attitude towards the Templars seems to have taken place about the time of the election of Pope Clement V in 1305—and perhaps it was the very election of a "puppet" pope which induced that change, by showing the French king a way in which he might be able to relieve his financial crisis by laying his hands on the Templars' wealth. The key to this plan was that Clement must be persuaded to use his spiritual authority by pronouncing the Templars as heretics: then everything could be made to fall into the king's hands. Clement therefore had a crucial role to play. And so the campaign began. What was required first of all was evidence of heretical practices among the Templars themselves, which could then be laid before to the supreme pontiff for his judgment.

Rumours relating to certain practices among the Knights were already rife in France, even if largely unfounded. Philip now did his best to fan those rumours. The fact that the Templars' chapter meetings were held in secret and at night proved a convenient pretext for a veritable hornet's nest of suspicions. It was said (though by whom it was never clear) that under the cover of secrecy "abominable practices" were regularly performed, especially during initiation rites for young knights entering the order. These practices included spitting on the crucifix, the worship of idols, and a variety of sexual acts including the kissing of the penis or anus of the Grand Master. Since the Templars were a body of men who had taken vows of chastity and had therefore rejected any association with the female sex, there were the inevitable charges of homosexuality.

In order to gather the evidence he needed Philip proceeded to infiltrate well-paid spies into the Templars' ranks. For two years he listened to every account of malpractice that was brought to his ears, carefully collating whatever suited his purpose. At the end of that time he felt ready to act. Accordingly in the spring of 1307 the king arranged a meeting with the recently-crowned pope, Clement V, who had been nursing grave ill-health in Bordeaux for the whole of the previous year, but who had now moved along with the papal court to Poitiers. And it was here that the two men met. It was the beginning of a power-struggle which was to decide the fate of the Knights Templar. The trap was being set.

To his credit Clement, presented with what passed as evidence of the Templars' guilt, remained unconvinced, and said so. He was proving to be not quite the pushover Philip had anticipated. The king promptly changed tactics. He began to bombard the pope with letters reiterating the accusations brought against the knights, and despatched ambassadors to Clement pressing the pontiff to take urgent action against them. In August of that year the Grand Master of the Templars, Jacques de Molay, who had been summoned by the pope from Cyprus to answer these accusations, persuaded Clement to order an official inquiry in accordance with the strict procedures of Canon Law.

This was not something King Philip felt able to agree to: he was certainly not prepared to risk an enquiry which might well have exonerated the Templars altogether by showing that all accusations had been based on evidence from entirely unreliable witnesses. Instead, the king took direct action. On 13 October, at his insistence all the Knights Templar in France were placed under arrest, and their property sequestered *in toto*. Among those arrested was the Grand Master himself, Jacques de Molay, who found himself facing a raft of charges based on the specious evidence of former knights who, as it transpired, had already been dishonourably expelled from the order, and were now simply seeking revenge.

Pope Clement, even though he enjoyed official jurisdiction over the Templars, was never once consulted over these sudden arrests. King Philip's chief minister, the same Guillaume de Nogaret who had prompted the attack on Pope Boniface at Anagni, now pronounced that the French king had acted perfectly legitimately in arresting the knights, on the grounds that he had merely acted at the request of the Inquisitor General after consultation with the pope. Neither claim possessed a single grain of truth.

One of the better moments of Clement's papacy followed. The pope wrote angrily to King Philip on 27 October, just two weeks after the mass arrest: "My dear son, we declare with sorrow that, in defiance of all rules, while we were far from you, you stretched forth your hand against the persons and goods of the Templars... You have committed outrages against the persons and goods of men who are immediately subject to me and to the Roman Church. In this hasty action all now see, and not without reasonable cause, an insulting scorn of us and of the Roman Church." These were surprisingly strong words. There is no surviving record of Philip's reply. There may never have been one. Instead the king resorted to that time-honoured method of extracting the information he needed from his prisoners—torture. And not surprisingly, within a very short time he had successfully obtained the confessions he required, including several from Jacques de Molay, though the Grand Master robustly denied all charges of sodomy.

What followed must have been hard to comprehend at the time, and has remained so ever since. Within a matter of weeks after hearing of these confessions Pope Clement issued a bull, *Pastoralis praeeminentiae*, ordering the arrest of all Templars throughout Christendom, and requiring their property to be held in the name of the church.

What can have caused quite so startling a *volte-face* has provoked volumes of speculation ever since: these vary from the charitable—that the pope believed the Templars had to be sacrificed for the sake of the wider interests of the church (whatever they might mean)—to the damning verdict that Clement simply buckled under the threats of the French king largely out of fear of a repetition of the Anagni outrage. What seems beyond question is that, whether as a result of pressure from King Philip or because he actually believed the confessions which Philip submitted to him that November, Clement managed to become convinced that the Templars were to some degree guilty of the charges put to them, and therefore deserved to be punished.

From this point onwards the battleground changes. The leading issue becomes not so much whether the Templars were innocent or guilty—because they were already a lost cause—as whether the French king or the pope was to have the decisive say in determining their fate. The Templars themselves were to become mere pawns in a shoddy power-game. We see Clement constantly altering his position, repeatedly attempting to assert some degree of authority, but repeatedly failing to do so, forever on the retreat, forever outmanoeuvred, growing weaker and weaker both in health and in will-power, desperately seeking some haven of peace but forever being dragged back to be bludgeoned yet again by his nemesis Philip the Fair.

Events unfolded with a predictable deadliness once Clement had called for the mass arrest of the Templars. Philip now felt he could do what he liked. The Paris Inquisition was in full swing, and by January 1308 almost 140 Templars who were arrested in Paris had confessed to the familiar trumped-up charges: devil-worship, spitting and urinating on images of Christ, having carnal relations with other Templars, even having plotted with the Infidel in order to bring about the loss of the Crusader Kingdom. This carnival of absurdity continued unchecked until in February the cardinals from the papal Curia, who were the pope's representatives at these gruesome proceedings, began to voice their disquiet and express their unwillingness to condemn the knights. A number of the accused, including the Grand Master himself, promptly took heart and revoked their confessions, claiming that these had been extracted under torture.

Under pressure from the cardinals the pope then made another of his changes of direction and ordered the suspension of the Inquisition's activities, pronouncing that henceforth he would deal with the matter personally by setting up a papal commission which would undertake to try those knights who had been accused. The French king reacted with fury. Every form of character assassination followed: hostile pamphlets, threats of one kind or another, legal pressure from Nogaret, even attempts at blackmail. Predictably the brow-beaten Clement eventually submitted to Philip's demands that the papal commission, which was eventually convened in November 1309, should consist predominantly of clerics who were known to be royal placemen.

Nevertheless, knights who by now had endured two years in prison, frequently tortured, continued to regard the papal commission as a last ray of hope. Many retracted their former confessions. Some were bold enough to admit to the treatment they had received in prison. "If I am made to suffer such torture again, I shall deny all that I am now saying, and tell you anything you wish," one knight assured those present. "I know in my heart that I would confess to anything," said another. "I would confess that I had killed God if they asked me."

For a while the trial appeared to be going well for the Templars. Nearly six hundred witnesses spoke up in their defence, while prosecution witnesses were few and for the most part incoherent. But the knights' hopes were soon dashed. A particularly robust defence of the Templars by two eminent priests proved too much for the prosecution: at the insistence of the king the Archbishop of Sens stepped in and ordered the entire proceedings of the commission to be overturned.

The pope did nothing. Fifty-four of the Templars on trial were pronounced guilty of heresy, and on the following morning, 12 May 1310, they were burnt at the stake outside the walls of Paris. Nine more knights followed them four days later. There was one final act in the drama. The French king wanted more than the death of a bunch of Templar heretics: he wanted the suppression of the entire Order. And in order to achieve this he needed a papal pronouncement to this effect. Clement, under the customary pressure from Philip, agreed to summon a general council of the church in order to settle the issue of the Templars once and for all. This was to meet at Vienne, to the south of Lyon on the banks of the River Rhône, but suitably outside French territory, so offering at least the appearance of impartiality.

The council finally assembled in October 1311, with more than a hundred bishops from all over Europe present. Proceedings dragged on month after month, as evidence of the Templars' supposed guilt was heard from all parts of the continent, until it became increasingly clear that the majority of the bishops present were either undecided or deeply reluctant to agree to the dissolution of the Order. Pope Clement, as ever, prevaricated. And no decision was reached. Then in March the following year the French king chose his moment: he descended on the by-now-exhausted body of clerics accompanied by a menacing troop of armed soldiers. And as always the pressure worked: within a matter of weeks more than three-quarters of the assembled bishops voted for the suppression of the Templars. And Clement issued his infamous bull, *Vox in excelso*, formally abolishing the Order.

There remained the question of what might be an appropriate punishment. In December 1313 Clement duly appointed a commission of three cardinals to decide on the fate of the leaders of the Templars, including the Grand Master. As a result in March 1314 Jacques de Molay and three others were condemned to perpetual imprisonment. Faced with this verdict the Grand Master turned on the pope in anger: "We are not guilty of those things of which we are accused, but we are guilty of having betrayed the Order to save our lives. The Order is pure; it is holy; the accusations are absurd and our confessions false."

De Molay and a fellow leader, Geoffrois de Charnay, were promptly handed over to the Provost of Paris. King Philip himself insisted they be put to death: and that very evening the two men were taken to the banks of the Seine where they were burnt at the stake within sight of the royal palace. De Molay cried out even as he burned that Pope Clement was an unjust judge.

§

During those soulful retreats from Avignon into the rural Comtat did Pope Clement ever suffer pangs of remorse over his betrayal of the Templars and his craven subservience to King Philip? And were there any regrets whenever the papal entourage rode past the Templars' *commanderie* with its lofty chapel in the heart of Avignon? If so, no such evidence survives.

One plausible, though slim, explanation exists for the pope's persistent sycophancy. Two months after issuing his papal bull abolishing the Templars' Order at the Council of Vienne Clement proclaimed a new crusade to the Holy Land, to be led by none other than King Philip the Fair. In order to finance such an enterprise the pope announced a ten per cent tax to be levied on all church income for the next six years. The following year King Philip took the cross—the crusader's symbol of commitment to the cause—from the hands of the papal nuncio in the presence of his three sons as well as his son-in-law, King Edward II of England. King Philip and Pope Clement were for once united in common purpose.

It is not entirely far-fetched to suggest that behind all the pope's vacillations and apparent feebleness over the previous six years lay a burning ambition that was soon to infect all the Avignon popes, which was to mount a final crusade to recapture the long-lost Bible lands and so liberate the holy city of Jerusalem from the "Infidel". To all the exiled popes this was to become a noble and passionate longing. And in the eyes of Clement V such a great venture could only possibly be achieved with huge funds from the church as well as the backing and leadership of the most powerful monarch in Christendom, King Philip the Fair of France.

Over the following year the ten per cent tax trickled into Avignon from a wide variety of countries. And it arrived in various forms: the tiny Christian settlement in Greenland paid its contribution in walrus teeth. Clement, pliant as ever, permitted most of the funds received to be paid directly to King Philip in order that he should be able to prepare his crusade. The money Philip received amounted to approximately five times the total annual income of the French monarchy. Not surprisingly the king was mightily grateful since the royal treasury was now able to pay off most of Philip's debts. Other sums of money never reached Avignon at all, but filled the pockets of local rulers—in England,

Castile, Aragon, Portugal, Majorca and no doubt elsewhere. Within a few years there would be other beneficiaries of that tax, among them a number of members of the pope's own family, the De Got, many of whom had already benefited greatly from the pope's nepotistic favours.

It was a less than glorious episode. And needless to say the crusade Clement dreamed of never took place.

§

The discreditable episode of the Knights Templar would almost certainly never have taken place had the papacy been able to remain in Rome, at a convenient distance from France, and with a pope who was Italian, not French. Without his resident "puppet" King Philip would never have got away with the incessant and belligerent pressure that he inflicted on Clement V. Away from the chaos of Italy it is true that the papacy had been able to find a renewed sense of security: but at a price. And the price to be paid was that all the Avignon popes, from Clement V onwards, found themselves increasingly drawn into the secular power struggles of northern Europe, particularly those between England and France in what was to become the Hundred Years War.

Along with the increasing secularization of the papacy went a growing materialism. Clement himself was partly responsible. He enjoyed money, and he enjoyed bestowing it on others, particularly those who could be of use to him. He openly practised simony: in other words he sold benefices. He was also responsible for introducing a tax of dubious justification whereby the first year's revenues from each one of those benefices he had sold were to go to the pope directly. So he profited both ways. Not surprisingly the papal treasury grew grotesquely large, far in excess of what a relatively small papal court in Avignon required for its needs.

On the other hand, many institutions, as well as people, benefited from his largesse. He created a university in Perugia. He established (somewhat surprisingly) chairs of Hebrew and Arabic in both Paris and Oxford universities. As for personal gifts, in addition to giving King Philip one-tenth of all church income in France to support his non-existent crusade, the pope made Philip numerous further gifts of money, as he also did the king of England as well as a large number of Clement's own relatives—because he practised nepotism just as openly as he did simony. No fewer than five of his family became cardinals.

A generous interpretation would be that all these practices—and malpractices—merely reflected the pope's need to shore up his position as the unchallenged spiritual leader of Christendom, free from the material anxieties and political threats that had beset his predecessors. Yet not everybody saw his behaviour in quite so favourable a light. One of the most vituperative of these was the poet Dante. At the time of Clement's election as pope Dante was in exile from his native Florence and under sentence of death. His crime was to have supported the party of the Holy Roman Emperor rather than that of the then pope, who at that time was Boniface VIII, the very pontiff who fell foul of Philip the Fair and was kidnapped at Anagni. A *coup d'état* mounted by the pope in Florence found Dante on the losing side. And losers were not treated kindly in medieval Italy.

Dante's credo was a conviction that the anarchic state of Italy could only be rectified by the Holy Roman Emperor exercising the traditional authority he had inherited from the days of Charlemagne. Only then could order be imposed on the warring factions throughout the Italian peninsula, and the disease of fragmentation ended. And when a youthful German prince, Henry of Luxembourg, was elected emperor in 1309 Dante was delighted that the ambitious young ruler received the fulsome support of none other than the new pope, Clement V, who within two months would be establishing his papal court in Avignon—temporarily only, as a mere staging-post on the way back to Rome, or so Dante firmly believed.

DANTE ALICHIERI

Rome was also the city where the young emperor was determined to be crowned. Accordingly he led an imperial army across the Alps, swept through Italy and finally achieved his ambition in the year 1312. But history then took a familiar turn. King Philip the Fair was less than happy about the election of a glamorous young German emperor: it was a role he would rather have liked for himself. He particularly disliked the prospect of a German ruler enjoying quite so much power in Italy.

As it transpired, and to the French king's advantage, the young emperor's bright star was already setting. In his campaign to suppress warring factions in Italy Henry had created numerous enemies, particularly in Florence. Above all there was a new opponent, a man who had hitherto supported the young emperor—Pope Clement V. Here was yet another change of heart by the Avignon pope. To those in papal circles it would not have come as a surprise: they had witnessed the pope's vacillations many times before. And the reason was the familiar one. At the same Council of Vienne at which Clement had signed the death warrant of the Templars, he was now persuaded by the French king to shift his allegiance from Henry to Philip's preferred candidate as emperor, King Robert of Naples who, it so happened, was a close relative of King Philip himself. Clement obediently complied. Within a year the Emperor Henry was dead, a victim of malaria, and Clement promptly awarded the imperial title to King Robert.

Dante felt this to be a cynical and self-interested betrayal: the pope had unforgivably changed sides. He duly erupted. And he did so in what was to become his most celebrated work, *The Divine Comedy*. This immensely long poem was to occupy Dante more or less continuously for the last twelve to fifteen years of his life, until shortly before his death in 1321. Its theme is the imaginary journey of a man (probably Dante himself) to visit souls in Hell, Purgatory and Paradise, guided by the Roman poet Virgil and by the imaginary Beatrice. It is in the cantos of the *Inferno*, and above all in the *Purgatorio*, where Dante unleashes his fury against Avignon and everything to do with it. He described events in biblical terms. Pope Clement was the Whore of Babylon. The removal of the papacy from Rome was the Babylonian Captivity, with the Mother Church being the one held captive and Rome the hapless widow. King Philip of France was Pontius Pilate, and elsewhere a malign giant.

Dante's vision of Avignon itself appears in *Purgatorio XXXII*:

Secure, like a fort on a high hill,
A loose whore sitting on top of it
Appeared to me, her eyes quick and bright
And, as though to keep her from being taken from him,
A giant, I saw, erect beside her,
And sometimes they kissed each other;
But because her greedy, wandering eye
She turned towards me, that fierce lover
Whipped her from her head down to her feet.

The image of Pope Clement as a greedy whore with a wandering eye is a crude version of what many of his contemporaries believed to be the truth, just as they believed that King Philip the Fair was indeed the possessive giant who whipped her into submission each time her eye wandered too far. It is doubtful if either Clement or King Philip were aware of Dante's insult at the time: none the less the poet's timeless fame has insured that posterity has preserved his verdict as a damning epitaph to both of them.

By the spring of 1314 Clement was dying. His last wish was to end his days in his native Gascony for which the rural Comtat had been a substitute all these years. Accompanied by a small personal retinue he set out from the papal city for the last time. He crossed the Pont St.-Bénézet to the far side of the Rhône, entering French territory under the threatening gaze of the castle and watchtower built by his patron and nemesis Philip the Fair. From here Clement turned north, following the course of the great river which had borne him to Avignon five years earlier. The road he took threaded its way between a steep limestone escarpment to the west and the swamps and marshlands of the ever-flooding Rhône. After some ten miles the party reached the castle of Roquemaure, a colossal bastion built on the edge of the Rhône (at the very place where 1,500 years earlier the Carthaginian general Hannibal had crossed with his 9,000 cavalry and thirty-seven elephants on his way to attack Rome). The castle, owned by a local lord whom Clement doubtless knew well, possessed defensive walls over thirteen feet thick and no fewer than seven fortified towers. Here the papal party rested. But it was to be as far as the pope could manage; his condition worsened, and on 20 April he died—it was said from eating a plate of ground emeralds prescribed by his doctor to alleviate his acute stomach pains.

Fragments of the castle of Roquemaure still exist scattered around the present-day town, including sections of the massive defensive walls and two of the seven towers, one of them perched uneasily on a rock so deeply eroded by centuries of wind and rain that it is now narrower than the tower it supports, resembling a huge stone apple-core.

Clement's death occurred barely one month after the Grand Master of the Templars, Jacques de Molay, whom he had entirely failed to protect, was burnt at the stake on the orders of the French king. Before the end of that same year King Philip himself was also dead, meeting his end as the result of a hunting accident. Perhaps a kind of rough justice had prevailed. The monarch who had so ruthlessly hunted down the Knights Templar, was himself finally hunted down.

St.-Agricol, one of the most handsome Gothic churches in the heart of Avignon, begun during the reign of John XXII, the second of the Avignon popes, and further embellished a century-and-a-half later.

3

Pope Midas

As soon as he heard of Clement's death Dante wrote to all the Italian cardinals beseeching them to press the Sacred College for an urgent return of the papacy to Rome. His views on the respective powers of the pope and Holy Roman Emperor once the "Babylonian Captivity" was over had been forcefully expressed in a political treatise issued the previous year, *De Monarchia*, "On Monarchy".

Dante cherished a vision of the Roman Empire (derived largely from his reading of Virgil) as a mighty force committed to pacifying and unifying the whole civilized world. For him this empire—Roman, Imperial and now Holy as well—provided the perfect model of a universal monarchy capable of lifting mankind out of chaos and establishing order and purpose, which of course for Dante meant the way of God. Accordingly he urged a political system in which sacred and material aims were inextricably entwined. Each should be dependent upon the other, and both be rooted in the same place co-existing side by side, in partnership. In his eyes establishing the papacy in Avignon contravened such an ideal in two important ways: not only was it a geographical separation from Rome, but Avignon's lust for secular as well as sacred power usurped a role that rightfully belonged to the Roman Empire. For these reasons it was vital that the papacy return to the Eternal City and abandon its worldly ambitions. The proper sphere of the church, after all, was the kingdom of God, not greedy earthbound kingdoms of mammon which should be left to temporal authorities to rule and squabble over. Such was Dante's angry blast against Avignon.

Unfortunately for the poet the majority of the cardinals failed to share his bright vision. The Italians were no longer the dominant group in the College of Cardinals: on his election in 1305 Clement V had straightaway appointed ten new members of the College of whom all but one were French (four of them being his own relatives), and in 1310 he had appointed five more, this time all of them French (two of them his nephews). The precise number of cardinals who made up the College at any one time is never entirely clear, but it was always well under a hundred, and the new appointments made by Clement during his papacy were certainly enough to shift the balance of power away from the Italians. In all, it would have been clear to those in the papal court in 1314 that Dante had become a voice crying in the wilderness. The likelihood of an immediate return to Rome, least of all the election of an Italian pope, was receding by the year.

At the time they received Dante's appeal the Italian cardinals had joined their French and others "in conclave" for the purpose of electing a pope to succeed Clement. They were not in Avignon, but had chosen to assemble along with the entire papal court in the ancient Celtic and Roman city of Carpentras, which was close to Avignon but considered to be a more congenial place of residence for a large body of churchmen. Furthermore Carpentras was on papal territory (which Avignon was not), being the administrative capital of the Comtat Venaissin, the papal county. It was home ground, though hardly safe home ground, as it turned out.

There followed one of the uglier consequences of the previous pope's nepotism. The cardinals whom Clement had appointed from his native Gascony, along with a group of supporters and hangers-on, incited an armed attack by hired mercenaries on the Italian faction in the papal Curia, doubtless fearing a diminution of their own power and influence now that their patron was dead. Riots broke out in Carpentras. There was bloodshed. Parts of the city were set on fire. Gangs roamed the streets. There was widespread looting by the Gascony supporters. A nephew of the late pope, who had been one of those responsible for the outbreak, made off with large sums of money from the papal treasury, and disappeared. Not surprisingly the conclave broke up and the Italian cardinals fled in fear of their lives. It was hardly the outcome Dante had wished for.

In an echo of the situation in Perugia after the death of Clement's predecessor, a period of deadlock ensued. There is no precise account of what went on in Carpentras, or in Avignon, over the many months that followed. The likeliest answer seems to be that nothing went on beyond a great deal of fruitless discussion accompanied by stubborn refusals to compromise on all sides. As a result, for two years Christendom had no pope to lead it, and church leaders remained incapable of agreeing on who should fill the void. In becoming truly international the College of Cardinals had now become truly impotent.

Then once again history repeated itself. The French king Louis X, son of Philip the Fair, finally in exasperation put pressure on the cardinals to meet on French territory, at Lyon, and here they duly assembled in March 1316. Two months later King Louis died, to be succeeded by his brother, who became Philip V. The new king had even less patience than his brother, and promptly ordered troops to besiege the divisive cardinals where they lodged in a Dominican convent, under instructions not to let any of them out until a pope had been elected, insisting also that the quantities of food and drink allowed into the place be reduced day by day until their job was done.

These draconian methods produced the desired result. One month later, on 7 August, a conclave of no-doubt-slimmer cardinals finally elected one of their own number. He was a diminutive and elderly cleric who was a former bishop of Avignon and, like his predecessor, was also a skilled lawyer, an expert in canon and civil law. He was Jacques Duèse, another Frenchman, a native of Cahors in the Quercy region of central France. The second Avignon pope took the name John XXII.

In several respects John turned out to be an unexpected figure as Supreme Pontiff. If the hungry cardinals locked up in a Lyon convent for all those weeks had conspired to elect John as little more than a stop-gap largely in order to win their freedom and a good meal, they were in for a great many surprises. One of the qualities that was to emerge in Pope John was a remarkable gift for longevity: he may have been well into his seventies at the time of his election, yet instead of fading quietly away decently soon he proceeded to live and rule vigorously—and often ruthlessly—for a further eighteen years.

In fact it was under Pope John during those eighteen years that the Avignon we recognize today began to take shape.

§

The lay-out of towns often remains substantially unchanged over centuries as if frozen by the passage of time, however much buildings themselves have become replaced and rebuilt. Streets and alleyways are arteries carrying the life-blood of a place throughout its history. This is true of Avignon, as it is of many other battle-scarred towns and villages in Provence. If you had a buzzard's eye gazing down at the modern city spread below you, the line of ramparts which King Louis destroyed as long ago as the early thirteenth century would still be clearly visible some distance within the shell of the expanded city, in the shape of four roads which link together to form a ring, the most prominent of them being the present-day Rue Vernet. These four roads encircle what was the original medieval city, and within that tight cordon everyone once lived, cheek by jowl, all five thousand of them. A fragment of those original medieval ramparts is still carefully preserved like some fossilized beast protruding from a modern wall at the intersection of the Rue Vernet and the Rue St.-Charles.

In October 1316, just two months after his election, the new pope moved into the bishop's palace high up on the Rocher des Doms close to the cathedral, where he had resided previously in the days when he had been Avignon's bishop.

It is almost from this moment that the city began to grow, spilling outwards from those former ramparts in an expanding labyrinth of narrow streets and hidden squares. Astonishingly the population of Avignon was to multiply to at least five times its former size during those eighteen years of John's papacy. Much of this expansion was the indirect result of the papal court having at last established itself in Avignon with an air of permanence now that the pope himself was installed here. The papacy seemed to have come to stay. This meant that there had to be comfortable houses for members of the court to live in: no longer the dingy lodgings which the papal entourage had been compelled to endure under Clement, and which had often driven them to seek accommodation in Carpentras, or elsewhere in the Comtat, or indeed anywhere that was preferable to the unhealthy squalor of the papal city.

The change in the city's fortunes was swift and dramatic. Avignon had long been poor: but now the papal court began to enrich the place beyond anyone's dreams. Most of the cardinals were men of considerable wealth in their own right, and very soon there was a rush of lavish spending aimed at making their lives more in tune with the privileged status they assumed to be their right. As for the papacy itself, spoils garnered from the estates of the now-disbanded Templars were a considerable addition to the papal income. Besides, taxes collected in the name of the papacy from all parts of the Christian world were beginning to take on the proportions of an avalanche. Pope John, a highly skilled lawyer, soon managed to create a vast and intricate fiscal system to the huge benefit of the papal treasury. These taxes came in a variety of forms: the most lucrative (as well as the most cunning) was a ten per cent levy on all income deriving from benefices which the pope himself had granted—from archbishoprics down to the appointment of village priests. This was a catchment which extended widely across Christian Europe. Not surprisingly the recipients of such benefices were only too eager to pay the required levy as an expression of gratitude for papal favours, many of the benefices being handsomely lucrative in themselves.

In consequence the papal treasury grew ever wealthier. One eye-witness in Avignon wrote: "Every time I went to the apartment of the Lord Pope's chamberlain I inevitably found bankers, money changers, tables loaded with gold, and clerks weighing and counting florins." It is hard not to believe that the man was reminded of the New Testament account of Christ driving the money-changers from the temple. When John became pope the treasury had been severely plundered by Clement's relatives after his death, as well as by his numerous gifts to the French king, and is known to have held no more than seventy thousand gold florins. By the end of John's papacy that same treasury is recorded as containing no less than eighteen million florins (one florin was approximately the price of a sheep), with a further seven million being the value of jewellery, gold and silver plate, church vessels, crosses, mitres, crowns and other precious object which the pope had assiduously stored away over the years. It is no accident that John was described as possessing the Midas touch.

The effect of such a flood of affluence on Avignon itself was massive, and it acted as a magnet to people right across the continent anxious to grab their share of it. Every possible service industry sprung up in the city, from banks to workshops and trading organizations of all kinds. Merely a year after the papal court settled in Avignon rich merchants from Florence were already establishing branches of their business in response to the demand for luxury goods: textiles, metalwork, jewellery, ivories, silverware, ornaments of all kinds, furs and fine clothing. Within a few years Avignon became the trading centre for the whole of Provence, and as a result it soon possessed a flourishing international community. A babel of languages could be heard in the streets and the squares, mingling with the local Provençal. There were German and Flemish confraternities established in the city, for the most part middlemen who traded between Italy and the north, using the Rhône as a highway for conveying goods north and south. There were architects from France designing the new houses for members of the court, painters from Tuscany decorating those houses, craftsmen from all parts of Europe furnishing them with everything that was needed, or else setting up stalls in the open to display their wares wherever there was space in the expanding city. At the same time, with so much money circulating, Italian banking houses began to proliferate: within three years of Pope John's arrival it is recorded that as many as 43 money-changers were operating within the city.

Situated at the gates of France and with easy access to Italy and the rest of the Mediterranean, Avignon seemed ideally placed to prosper. And it did so. But where did all this money go? There were innumerable luxuries, of course. Some of these were relatively modest; the pope established a small private zoo containing animals from all parts of the known world—lions, camels, bears and wild cats among them. Other luxuries were more in keeping with the status of the ruler of all Christendom. The papal entourage, in addition to an army of secretaries and servants, included more than one hundred squires who were required to be in attendance on the pontiff should he require their presence. The papal chamberlain was always on hand to assist the pope with the pontiff's garments and mitre, and to place on his feet the papal slippers which visitors to His Holiness would be required to kiss.

Displays of sumptuous clothing generally were beginning to become part of daily life throughout the papal court, extending to the ladies who could now enjoy the privilege of wearing silks and ermine, embellished with jewellery and gold and silver ornaments.

And yet there can have been few opportunities for grandiose ceremonial occasions during these early years of the papacy since there was nowhere in Avignon magnificent enough in which to hold them. Until the building of the papal palace several years later, and the splendid mansions of the cardinals, court life would have remained a relatively piecemeal affair.

By no means all the new wealth merely lined the pockets of the cardinals or swelled the coffers of the papal treasury. Pope John cherished a number of long-term ambitions, all of which would require funds in plenty. Hopes of launching yet another crusade to "liberate" the Holy Land still flickered in Avignon, sometimes strongly, more often fitfully. One essential step in this direction was to finance an army to recover the lost papal territories in Italy from Bologna southwards. Such a campaign, if successful, would open up the possibilities of such a crusade, as well as preparing the way for the realization of that other persistent dream, the eventual return of the papacy to Rome.

These projects were all to remain dreams. None the less John's view of what was required of the papacy at such a turbulent moment in history was strictly realistic. In the words of the most distinguished modern writer on the Avignon papacy, Professor Guillaume Mollat: "In the 14th century no power, even one essentially spiritual, could rule the world unless it was able to enforce its actions by the possession of territories and financial prosperity." In Dante's view, by adopting this materialistic role Avignon was usurping what was rightfully the responsibility of the Holy Roman Empire. But then Pope John was the last person to have seen eye to eye with Dante. He was a man dedicated to grabbing whatever he could in the name of the papacy.

On the other hand there were a number of John's peaceful endeavours which did bear fruit. He used some of the spoils of the Templars to found religious orders in Spain and Portugal. He promoted missionary activity in the Middle East and Asia, establishing bishoprics as far distant as India. He established a university in his native town of Cahors. And in his adopted city, Avignon, he founded the papal library, which has continued to this day, though long ago returned to the Vatican in Rome. More surprisingly for a man often seen as a miser, John set up an office of good works, called the Pignotte, where food, clothing and medicines were regularly handed out to the poor and needy. From a large building on what is still called the Place Pignotte, close to the former ramparts on the east side of the city, nearly 70,000 loaves of bread used to be distributed every week during the entire eighteen-year span of John's reign.

But the most conspicuous use of Avignon's new riches was in building. Soon after he moved into the old bishop's palace in October 1316 Pope John proceeded to buy up a whole area of neighbouring houses high up on the Rocher des Doms in order to expand the palace. He was also responsible for one of the most elegant of Avignon's early Gothic churches, St. Agricole, named after an unlikely-sounding saint who was actually an early bishop and one of the patron saints of the city. The church was embellished a century and a half later by a handsome carved portico and a broad flight of stone steps leading up to it. Just across the street was the former Templars' chapel and *commanderie* which by now were in the possession of that other order of crusader knights, the Hospitallers or Knights of St. John of Jerusalem. As Pope John gazed across from his new church towards the chapel where the Templars had so recently worshipped, did he ever, one wonders, harbour doubts about his predecessor's treatment of the hapless knights? Or was the hard-bitten pragmatist in him content to watch the river of history flow impassively by, bringing with it, as it did, such a gratifying share of the Templars' wealth ?

Within two years of John establishing the papal court on a permanent basis the first of the huge cardinals' mansions, soon to be such a dominant feature of the city, had risen almost under the shadow of the twelfth-century cathedral. Known today as the Petit

Palais (later greatly embellished by a Renaissance façade), it was built by one of the French cardinals as a residence for himself and what must have been a retinue on a princely scale. It was constructed on three floors round a Gothic courtyard of an elegant simplicity which suggests the dominant influence of Cistercian monastic architecture, with its emphasis on purity of line and the total absence of decoration. After the owner died a few years later the palace was bought in 1323 and enlarged still further by another cardinal, Arnaud de Via, one of the pope's nephews who had been appointed, and greatly enriched, by the familiar practice of nepotism which John favoured just as strongly as did his predecessor.

Not content with possessing one of the few monumental residences in Avignon at that time, Cardinal de Via spread his ambitions wider still. On the far side of the Rhône across the Pont St.-Bénézet lay the "ville neuve", or "new town" which King Philip the Fair had founded thirty years earlier as a strategic frontier post guarding the great bridge that linked France with Avignon and Provence. In typically aggressive fashion Philip had announced his presence here by constructing a castle bristling with turrets overlooking the river (of which one solitary tower still stands, the Tour Philippe-le-Bel). It was in this "new town" of Villeneuve-lès-Avignon that Arnaud de Via became the first of the Avignon cardinals to take advantage of the wide-open spaces on the far side of the river to build expansive palaces for themselves and their ever-growing crowd of retainers. (Within a few decades there would be as many as fifteen of these huge mansions in Villeneuve, known as *livrées* because the land on which they were built had been "relinquished" by their previous owners without, one suspects, having been given much choice in the matter.)

Cardinal de Via began building his *livrée* in 1330, probably as a summer palace, and it was completed in 1333, two years before his death. The private chapel he built, and in which he is buried, became the Collegiate Church of Nôtre-Dame and subsequently the town's parish church, which it is to this day. The nearby

Musée Municipal displays a touching link with the cardinal in the form of a small ivory statue of the Virgin and Child which he donated to his church (and very likely commissioned), the group shaped in a delicate curve for the simple reason that it was carved from a single elephant's tusk.

Pope John was not one to be outdone by his opulent nephew. For his own summer residence he chose—wisely— not to stray on to French territory but to remain securely on the eastern bank of the Rhône. In 1321 he built a huge turreted palace a short distance north of Avignon with an accompanying pleasure-garden leading down to the river at Sorgues. We know the name of the architect, Pierre de Gauriac, but that is almost all we know. Of John's summer palace only insignificant fragments remain.

But a few miles further north another of John's mansions has survived, at least in part (and would have survived totally had the retreating German army not dynamited it on 20 August 1944). This was one of the first building projects the pope undertook, beginning in 1316: and it seems significant that it should have been so because it represents one of the private passions for which John became noted— and sometimes vilified—namely, wine. He built his "new chateau", Châteauneuf, high above the valley of the Rhône among vineyards which his predecessor had planted, but had never lived to enjoy. It is hard to estimate today how extensive were the papal vineyards of

Châteauneuf-du-Pape; in the succeeding centuries the place has grown to become the centre of one of the most prestigious wine industries of southern France, and the papal insignia of mitre and keys is displayed on many a bottle whose contents never came from papal lands.

At least there can be no doubt about the location and scale of the original papal vineyards because fragments of the boundary wall still enclose what is described as the "Clos des Papes". The long circuit of the original perimeter wall makes an evocative walk into the Middle Ages. On this high ridge above the Rhône valley suddenly no one is around: there is nothing except the wind tearing at this lone and crumbled wall, with the occasional glimpse of John's castle through gaps in the stonework, and in one place a massive broken arch against the skyline under which Pope John would so very many times have passed. The Museum of Wine in Châteauneuf itself displays one exhibit which is almost as evocative: an object which offers more than a hint at the famous papal thirst for wine. This is a gargantuan oak cask of the fourteenth century, blackened with age, and capable of holding four thousand litres of wine.

A more personal record of Pope John's appetite for the good things of life has come down to us in the form of a list of requirements for a banquet he gave to guests and members of the papal court on 22 November 1324 as a celebration of the marriage of his great-niece. The list reads as follows: 4,012 loaves of bread, 9 oxen, 55 sheep, 8 pigs, 4 wild boars, large but unspecified quantities of various fish, 200 capons, 690 chickens, 3,000 eggs, 580 partridges, 270 rabbits, 40 plovers, 37 ducks, 59 pigeons, 4 cranes, 2 pheasants, 2 peacocks, 292 small birds, 3 hundredweight of cheese, 2,000 apples and other fruit, 11 barrels of wine (doubtless of the scale of the example above).

§

Not everyone liked Pope John. To be seen as an authoritarian lawyer and miser on the one hand, and a wine-loving hedonist on the other, cannot have made it easy for those around him to understand or warm to the man. He was not noted for his charm. By all accounts his manner towards subordinates was often imperious and intemperate, while his restless and intrusive energy would have been disconcerting to those in the papal court who might well have felt that someone of his advanced years should be taking life a little more calmly, particularly in the wake of the chaos that had followed the death of Pope Clement.

John's nepotism also aroused enmity. Even by the standards of the day it was considered excessive. During the eighteen years of his papacy John created twenty-eight cardinals, twenty being from southern France, eight of them from his native diocese of Cahors, three being his own nephews. In addition a large number of needy relatives were awarded lucrative posts in the church administration. It was this reputation for favouring his own circle which came close to bringing about his downfall at the very outset of his papacy, when he almost became the victim of a bizarre episode of sorcery instigated by the bishop of his home town of Cahors. In a bid to murder the newly-elected pope and thereby dispose of his band of followers the bishop arranged for wax images to be placed in the chapel of the archbishop's palace at Toulouse, each figure bearing a strip of parchment inscribed with the words "May Pope John die." Further wax figures were hidden within loaves of bread which were then delivered by bearers to Avignon. Not surprisingly their arrival on this improbable mission aroused suspicion in the papal city, and the men were arrested. They duly inculpated the bishop, who was himself promptly arrested. He then confessed to having tried to assassinate the pontiff "by poison and by sorcery with wax images, ashes of spiders and toads, the gall of a pig, and like substances." The man was flayed alive and finally roasted over a slow fire.

By far the most testing conflict of John's papacy was with the Franciscans. The issue over which battle lines were drawn sounds like one of those vapid theological debates akin to "how many angels can balance on the head of a pin?" The key point of dispute was: did

Christ and his disciples own property? One branch of the Franciscan Order known as the Spirituals maintained that they did not. Pope John claimed that there was scriptural evidence to prove that they did.

The argument progressed far beyond mere theological swordplay. The pope denounced the Spirituals as heretics, handing over many of their number to the Inquisition, thereby condemning them to be burnt at the stake, which a great number were, including women who were sisters of the Order of St. Francis. The response of the Spirituals was no less extreme; they maintained that the church as represented by the Avignon papacy had become a victim of avarice, pride and delights of the flesh, that it was the new Babylon, the Great Whore, and the pope was Antichrist.

The Franciscans were a mendicant (i.e. a begging) religious order committed to a life of austerity and poverty as prescribed in the rule of life composed by their founder St. Francis of Assisi a century earlier. It is easy enough to understand why the plutocracy and conspicuous greed of the Avignon papacy should have appeared to the Franciscans to be entirely incompatible with any kind of spiritual life. But it is equally easy to understand how a pope who enjoyed hosting banquets with four thousand loaves of bread and eleven gargantuan barrels of wine might be disinclined to subscribe to a rule of poverty. The academic dispute over whether or not Christ and his disciples could be proved to have owned property may have been little more than a convenient bludgeon with which either side could batter the other. And yet the underlying issue was a matter of the most profound importance to both sides. If it was acceptable for the church to own goods, then the mendicants were little more than deluded beggars. If it was not acceptable, then the entire worldly edifice of the church, with its palaces, its gold and its glitter, was no more than the manifestations of the new Babylon.

It was in February 1317, a mere six months after his election as pope, that John prepared to issue his papal bull excommunicating the Spirituals, summoning their leaders to appear before him in Avignon.

At first those who were charged and handed over to the Inquisition to meet their fate were small fry. But in the years that followed the cause of the Spirituals became championed by far more substantial figures within the church. One of these was a Franciscan theologian and logician from the University of Oxford, William of Ockham. Pope John, in his relentless determination to root out all forms of unorthodoxy, summoned William to Avignon, apparently in order to elucidate certain heretical views which the Englishman held on the subject of transubstantiation. William duly arrived in the papal city in 1324, where he took up residence in a convent, remaining semi-captive in the city more or less at the pope's pleasure. It was here three years later that he met up with another "rebel": this was one of the most contentious churchmen of his day, Michael of Cesena, who was nothing less than the head (known as the "general") of the entire Franciscan Order. Michael too had been summoned to Avignon by the pope, in his case to answer pertinent questions about his views on the vexed question of whether Christ and his apostles could be said to have owned goods.

Michael and Pope John were soon at loggerheads, and their relationship deteriorated rapidly. Meanwhile William of Ockham, instructed by his Franciscan superior to study a number of bulls the pope had issued on the subject of poverty, declared after a careful reading of them that they contained so many errors that the pope had showed himself to be himself a heretic. The "more than stern doctor", as William had been described by a colleague, had evidently been incensed by the pope's capricious twisting of biblical texts in an attempt to substantiate what was a thoroughly flimsy argument, and did not hesitate to say so. The fastidious logician had taken on the cunning lawyer.

Needless to say, to pronounce that the pope was a heretic within the walls of his own city was tantamount to signing a death warrant for both himself and Michael of Cesena. They had already been forbidden to leave Avignon without papal permission; now, sensing that their arrest must surely be imminent, both men made the decision to flee. Together they slipped out of the city by night, and made their way to Marseille, and thence by ship to Italy.

By this time hostility to the pope was also building up in the person of the newly-elected Holy Roman Emperor, Louis (or Ludwig) of Bavaria. John had opposed Louis' election and forbidden him to exercise his imperial authority until he, as pope, permitted it. Louis retaliated by denying that the pope had any authority whatsoever over imperial elections, and then attacked his persecution of the Spirituals. Ignoring Pope John's summonses to appear in Avignon under threat of excommunication, Louis provocatively marched with an army southwards to Rome where in January 1328 he was ceremonially crowned emperor in the former papal city in St. Peter's itself, a procession having conducted him there mounted on a white charger and clothed entirely in white.

Not content with this multiple rebuff to the pope in Avignon, three months later Louis pronounced John deposed as pope by imperial decree. A hurriedly assembled body of sundry priests and laymen were persuaded by the emperor to elect in his place an "anti-pope" who—to rub salt deeper still in John's wounds—was a Franciscan monk sympathetic to the heretical Spirituals. He was an Italian, Pietro Rainalducci, who took the papal title Nicholas V. The appointment signalled to the Christian world the fact that the Holy Roman Emperor was now a champion of the Spirituals, and that the Avignon pope's condemnation of them meant nothing at all. Accordingly it was under Louis' protection that Michael of Cesena and William of Ockham, having fled Avignon, now chose Rome as a place to settle. William was reputed to have said to the emperor on the occasion of their first meeting: "Do you defend me with your sword, and I will defend you with my pen."

If there was ever to be a conclusive trial of strength for the Avignon papacy, it was surely now. What actually occurred during the following two years was indeed a startling demonstration of just how formidably powerful was the voice of an elected pope, whether he was Italian or French, in Rome or in Avignon. Louis as it turned out had no weapons to match. He could rely only on temporal power, and in a very short time that grip on temporal power was shown to be extremely weak. He proved himself unable to stabilize order either in Italy or among the numerous warring factions in his native Germany. As a result, a mere year after his arrival in Rome Louis decided to retreat north to Germany. It is unclear what happened to Michael of Cesena after Louis' departure, but William of Ockham soon joined the emperor in Munich where he remained a luminary, continuing to fire broadsides against the pope right up until his death twenty years later. It has been suggested that in the end he became reconciled with the Avignon papacy, a claim supported by no convincing proof.

Meanwhile support for the puppet anti-pope Nicholas V, deprived of his protector and by now excommunicated along with his emperor, rapidly withered away. In a rare example of clemency Pope John assured him of a pardon, perhaps on the grounds that the innocent monk had merely been the victim of Louis' overbearing ambitions. Nicholas then took himself to Avignon where in August 1330 he formally renounced his claim to the papacy.

It was the end of a battle which John at one stage had seemed likely to lose. The influence of the German emperors on the affairs of Italy was never to be so strong again. The stabilizing imperial presence which had been so passionately longed for by Dante was a fading dream never to return. Meanwhile the sad anti-pope Nicholas remained in what may be described as "benevolent imprisonment" in Avignon for a further three years until his death in October 1333, his benevolent jailer Pope John surviving him by just fourteen months.

*The pope who began to make Avignon rich: John XXII,
who reigned until his nineties.*

4

Cardinal Virtues

and Vices

If Pope John vastly enriched Avignon during his eighteen-year reign, then his cardinals enriched themselves no less lavishly, and sometimes even more so. Whereas popes had global matters to engage in and sometimes to finance—wars, crusades, religious foundations to sponsor, impecunious monarchs to support—the cardinals were by and large free to spend their wealth on themselves. And many of them did so in style. Surviving wills and inventories testify to the splendour in which they lived. Their wealth derived from a variety of sources. Many of them had already received handsome gifts from the pope, more accurately described as bribes designed to facilitate his election. Then there was a steady flow of income from the numerous benefices which they had been awarded, or bought. A cardinal would frequently hold not just a single benefice but several, reaping his share of taxes gleaned from each of them even when he might rarely, if ever, have set foot in the places concerned. There were also lucrative taxes drawn from the towns and villages across the papal county, the Comtat Venaissin; without being required to contribute materially to the wellbeing of the region, the cardinals were still entitled to half the entire revenues received from the Comtat, the other half swelling the coffers of the papal treasury.

The lives they led matched their wealth. Even before they settled in Avignon and Villeneuve their gastronomic excesses had become legendary. A banquet was reputedly held for Clement V in Carpentras, the feast being concluded with candied and crystallised fruits, made in the nearby town of Apt, which the guests were invited to pluck from miniature trees made of pastry, these being supplemented with little sugary sweets decorated with threads of golden caramel. (To this day a Carpentras speciality is a crunchy multi-coloured sweet streaked with threads of sugar, known as *berlingots*, the word being—at least according to legend—a corruption of Pope Clement's name, Bertrand de Got.)

It is hardly surprising that when Pope John took issue with the Franciscan Spirituals over the question of poverty, not a single cardinal is known to have voiced his support for the Spirituals.

But if the cardinals represented the "inner circle" of the papal court, numerically they formed only a small part of it. The court is known to have consisted of at least four hundred people, all of whom were salaried, and all of whom received in addition their clothing, lodgings and day-to-day expenses *gratis*. The pope's private chapel alone was attended by no fewer than thirty chaplains. For a place which only a decade or so earlier had been modestly poor and distinctly run-down the change was dramatic. It has been estimated that by the end of John's papacy the papal court cost approximately ten times as much to maintain as the French royal court in Paris. In the words of Professor Mollat: "The papal court outshone all the other courts of Europe by the extravagance of its living and the splendour of its feasts."

Such opulence reflects not just the enormous wealth acquired by the Avignon papacy, particularly under Pope John, but also points to the size and complexity of the papal administration; this was to a large extent the product of the legal training which all the Avignon popes received, and which had already made the city into a lawyer's paradise. Yet this complex administration was still in an embryonic state, only becoming a smoothly-working piece of machinery under later popes, particularly after the completion of that gigantic labyrinth which is the Papal Palace. For the time being, under Pope John the weighty business of running Christendom was still somewhat makeshift, operating as best it could depending on what space could be found to accommodate so much legalistic bureaucracy.

Fortunately Pope John showed himself to be a formidable administrator. His studies in canon and civil law in Orléans and Paris as a younger man now stood him in good stead, as did his years as chancellor to the king of Naples shortly before he became a cardinal in the year 1312. There can be no doubt that after the financial shambles left behind by his predecessor, and the eighteen-month hiatus that followed Clement's death, John succeeded in leaving the affairs of the Avignon papacy in an extremely healthy state. It was now exceptionally rich and well on the way to becoming exceptionally well-organized as well.

Historians inclined to be generous towards Pope John have maintained that all these rigorous endeavours were motivated by a single great dream—that of the ultimate crusade designed to drive the forces of Islam from the Holy Land and so "liberate" Jerusalem. Certainly, on his election John had followed the example of his predecessor and declared his intention to launch such a crusade as soon as possible. He also (again like his predecessor) granted the French king yet more money in order to pay off his debts and thereby free the monarch to play a leading part in promoting a military expedition. The fact that in all the eighteen years of John's papacy no crusade ever materialized may suggest that he was better at dreams than actions. And in this respect he was not alone; noblemen throughout Europe were forever taking the cross and vowing loudly to set sail for the Holy Land, only to discover any number of good reasons for not actually doing so. On the other hand it may be fairer to Pope John to say that without peace being brokered between France and England, and without the re-establishment of papal control of territories in Italy, neither of which John was able to achieve, no large-scale military expedition to the Bible lands could ever have been successfully mounted.

What remains beyond doubt is that Pope John's vision of what was required of Christendom in these uncertain times—money or political muscle—was the product of a huge apprehension of the growing menace of Islam. Everywhere Christian leaders looked it seemed that Muslim banners were being raised. The crusader kingdom in the Holy Land had finally collapsed with the fall of Acre in 1291. There was the rising Turkish threat to the whole of the eastern church, as well as to the Balkan countries in eastern Europe over which the Turks were increasingly establishing their rule. There was also the continued presence of Islam in southern Spain, in the form of the Moorish kingdom of Granada.

One direct consequence of this threat from beyond the borders of Christendom was a determination by church authorities, led by the papacy, to root out the enemies lurking within its borders. Any kind of deviation from orthodoxy began to be seen as a dangerous luxury no longer to be tolerated. All forms of heresy needed to be crushed. It was as if orthodoxy itself was becoming a kind of religion. And Pope John was one of its high priests.

The most turbulent of his campaigns to eliminate heresy within the church had been the battle with the Franciscan Spirituals, which ended with the surrender and humiliation of the anti-pope Nicholas V and the inglorious departure back to Germany of the Holy Roman Emperor Louis of Bavaria who had appointed him. But there was another campaign against heresy being fought at this time, and it was one which involved Avignon particularly closely since the two people responsible for rooting out the heretics were both of them friends and associates of Pope John, one of whom was to become his immediate successor. The two men were the inquisitors Bernard Gui and Jacques Fournier.

Their victims were the last of the Cathars. The dualist faith of the Cathars rested on the belief (outlined in Chapter One) that the world was created not by God alone but by God and the Devil, God being responsible for matters of the spirit and the Devil for the material world. More than half a century earlier the Cathar church had seemingly been brought to an end in the year 1244 with the mass suicide of its leaders, the so-called *perfecti*, during the last-ditch siege of their mountain stronghold of Montségur in the northern foothills of the Pyrenees. This was the so-called Albigensian Crusade, which had been sponsored by the French crown and the papacy (still in Rome), and which appeared to have eliminated the heresy.

It was not entirely so. The Cathar faith had in fact survived, not on a large scale and mainly in a pocket of remote mountain villages close to the Spanish border, a region known as the Sabartès. Motives for the persistence of Cathar beliefs seem to have been as much political as spiritual; here were small and fairly poor rural communities with a profound dislike of the overbearing pride and arrogance of the orthodox church, and in particular of the undue weight of taxes imposed upon them by that church. The centre of this disaffection was the small village of Montaillou, at nearly four thousand feet in altitude and with a population of little more than two hundred. The church authorities had for some time turned a blind eye to certain unorthodox beliefs that were held in what was a relatively insignificant area of Languedoc. Pre-eminent among those beliefs was that the world had not been created by a single god; also that Jesus Christ could not possibly have existed as a creature of flesh and blood, and therefore his supposed crucifixion was a mere myth.

Such heretical beliefs, largely ignored up to now by the Catholic authorities presumably on the grounds that a few remote mountain villages were scarcely worth bothering about, suddenly seemed intolerable. And in the growing mood of zealous orthodoxy the new institution of the Inquisition turned its venom on this rural community of simple farmers. The campaign against them had begun in the summer of 1308 when on the orders of the inquisitor of Carcassonne, and on the pretext of unpaid livestock tithes, every man and woman in Montaillou over the age of twelve was arrested while (ironically) they were all assembled in celebration of the Feast of the Virgin.

This was merely the first warning shot; from now on Montaillou and the surrounding district were under the unforgiving eye of the church authorities operating as representatives of the Avignon papacy. The newly-appointed Chief Inquisitor was a man to whom history has awarded a dark and chilling reputation (though in part this is due to his being the sinister anti-hero of one of the great historical novels of recent times, Umberto Eco's *The Name of the Rose*). The Inquisitor was Bernard Gui. And over the next fifteen years this man is known to have summoned nearly 1,000 supposed "heretics" to appear before him at the Hôtel de l'Inquisition, which was a Dominican convent in Toulouse. A mere 139 of those accused were acquitted, while about 300 were given light sentences more as a warning than a punishment. The remainder were found guilty and compelled—if they were fortunate—merely to display the yellow cross of the heretic sewn on to their outer garment, while those less fortunate were condemned to life imprisonment or to be burnt at the stake. During these trials, if they can be called that, Gui refused to allow any of the accused to be represented by a lawyer (as they would have been entitled to in Common Law), insisting on the proceedings being conducted, in his words, "without the noise of advocates". The phrase appears in a directory which he wrote for the guidance of other inquisitors, *Practica officii inquisitionis heretice pravitatis*.

Gui was in his element punishing sinners. Umberto Eco may not have been far from the truth when he wrote of his fictional version of the man that he was "interested not in discovering the guilty, but in burning the accused." And the keenness with which he rooted out "heretics" was matched by the ruthlessness with which he extracted confessions from them. It is unlikely to have been a coincidence that in 1317 Pope John felt the need to issue an instruction to his inquisitors "limiting the use of torture" during trials for heresy.

Maybe the Inquisitor's zeal ultimately proved too much in the eyes of the Avignon pope, because in 1319 we hear of John instructing a different cleric to open proceedings against two men and a woman in the area of Montaillou who were being accused of consulting demons and making images for magical practices. In 1323 Gui was removed far from the torrid scene of his Inquisition, being appointed by Pope John to a bishopric in distant Galicia, in north-west Spain. He did return to Languedoc just one year later as Bishop of Lodève, but by this time the role of Chief Inquisitor had been filled by a former colleague who, like Gui, was a friend of Pope John. He was Jacques Fournier, who was a Cistercian monk.

It happens that we know more about Fournier, and the way he dealt with those brought before him, than we do about any other proceedings of the Inquisition at that time, the reason being that for ten years he kept a register of everything that was told him in the course of almost six hundred interrogations. And that register, which finally made up three massive tomes, went straight to Avignon for Pope John to absorb and approve.

Fournier by this time had left his Cistercian monastery to become Bishop of Pamiers, which was a recently-created bishopric in the Ariège district whose diocese included the mountain region of surviving Cathar villages, Montaillou among them. For the local Inquisition to be located here rather than in relatively distant Toulouse or Carcassonne meant that the eyes of the Inquisitor could now be more sharply focussed on this main area of heresy, where witnesses as well as suspects were conveniently close at hand.

Hence it was at the Bishop's Palace in Pamiers that Fournier set about conducting his meticulous interrogations, noting down every detail of every testimony he received. His curiosity about the daily lives of those he questioned bordered on the obsessive; nothing that came to his ears was allowed to slip away unrecorded, however irrelevant it might seem to the issue of heresy. As a result the Fournier Register (which is the source of the remarkable 1975 social study by Emmanuel Le Roy Ladurie, called simply *Montaillou*) is a document unique in its time, and highly unusual in any other time. It is effectively the biography of a village, compiling a detailed and intimate account of day-to-day life in a medieval pastoral community, with its hardships and its feuds, its loves and betrayals, jealousies and intrigues, and its struggles with the inclement mountain climate, all against the background of a tense religious conflict which is itself a matter of life and death.

Apart from a ruined castle on the hilltop little remains of medieval Montaillou, merely its ground-plan of houses and streets that are eerily shaped in the grassy hillside like an abandoned graveyard. The modern village, turning its back on a dark past, has been rebuilt a short distance away. Only a few villagers' surnames remain the same as those in the Fournier Register.

Always present in the background of the Montaillou story is Pope John's Avignon. It was the pope's personal mission which the Inquisitor was fulfilling at Pamiers; hence the ultimate seat of authority and judgment lay in Avignon itself. And when in 1320 Fournier struck the final blow at Montaillou by throwing the local priest into prison, it was in the name of that papal authority that he did so.

In the end the last of the Cathars condemned themselves, largely through their own words. In telling Fournier with complete lack of guile about their lives and their beliefs they inevitably offered up whatever evidence the Inquisitor needed. And at times it seemed that the accused no longer cared about the outcome. They knew that they were doomed to die. One of the Cathar *perfecti* by the name of Belbasto responded to his interrogator's questioning with these words: "There are four great devils ruling over the world: the lord Pope, who is the major devil I call Satan: the lord King of France is the second devil; the Bishop of Pamiers the third; and the Lord Inquisitor of Carcassonne the fourth."

There was small mercy for the last of the Cathars. They were disposed of unceremoniously. There was little of the sense of triumphant occasion that had attended the deaths of the earlier Cathars in the century before, when 183 "heretics" had been burnt at the stake in front of five bishops and the King of Navarre, the spectacle being described by one chronicler as a "holocaust, very great and pleasing to God". Again, as with the destruction of the Knights Templar, one is drawn to wonder if history might have recorded a different story had the papacy been far away in Rome rather than a relatively short distance from the little mountain villages of the Ariège. The pope might never even have heard of Montaillou, and its inhabitants might have gone on enjoying the pleasures of the flesh which Satan had so thoughtfully provided before allowing themselves to be reclaimed by God at the last gasp.

As it was, the tale was a far sadder one, though not of course for Jacques Fournier. His mission accomplished, he was duly created a cardinal by Pope John in 1327. Seven years later the pope himself finally succumbed to the grim reaper whose attentions he had successfully held at bay for so long, dying at the age of around ninety. The cardinals, who would have known Fournier well from his frequent visits to Avignon and his long friendship with Pope John, duly elected him as John's successor in 1334. The new pope chose to be called Benedict XII. Fortunately for his memory it is a name less associated in history with the man who obliterated the last of the Cathars than with the pontiff who began that hulk of a fortress which so awesomely symbolizes the might as well as the vulnerability of the Avignon papacy, the Palace of the Popes.

The tower of the private palace (livrée) built by the most flamboyantly wealthy of the Avignon cardinals, Annibale di Ceccano.

5

Palaces and Petrarch

A stone's-throw to the east of what is now Avignon's main thoroughfare, the Rue de la République, rises a grim tower of pale limestone with minimal windows high up beneath the battlements and no entrance of any kind at ground level. In the early-fourteenth century this lump of a bastion would have loomed massively over the squat tenements of the medieval city: a symbol of awesome power and unassailable authority. The tower was built as part of the *livrée*, or private palace, of one of the most flamboyantly wealthy of the Avignon cardinals, Annibale di Ceccano, and it was occupied by him and his extensive household throughout the papacy of Pope Benedict XII.

The fact that the place was built as a fortress as well as a palace explains a great deal about the state of mind of its occupants at this time. It demonstrates that there were dangerous enemies of the papacy not far away, in particular the Holy Roman Emperor, Louis of Bavaria. Louis had publicly declared Benedict's predecessor, Pope John XXII, deposed as a heretic, and in turn had been excommunicated by John for his pains. The feud between Louis and the papacy still smouldered, and in consequence neither the pope nor his cardinals could feel entirely safe from attack in their newly-adopted city, particularly since Avignon still had no adequate defensive fortifications. Louis, who not long ago had marched on Rome with an army, might conceivably decide at any time to march on Avignon.

On the other hand, the fact that such a massive palace as the Livrée Ceccano was being built at all demonstrates a general belief among the cardinals that in spite of such physical dangers the papacy was none the less here to stay: Avignon was no longer a mere transit camp on the road to Rome; besides which the Italian cardinals were now outnumbered by the French, for the majority of whom any return to Italy would have meant nothing less than exile. In fact Avignon was fast becoming the new Rome, in the process being transformed from a modest provincial town into a city of great mansions.

Today the Livrée Ceccano is the city's public library, with remarkable holdings of nearly 7,000 manuscripts and some 60,000 drawings and prints, mostly the spoils of French Revolutionary raids on local churches and monasteries. The building itself became a Jesuit college in the sixteenth century and a secondary school in the nineteenth, the result in both cases being the preservation of much of the detailing of the original palace—in particular the former ceremonial chamber decorated with the repeated motif of the cardinal's coat-of-arms, and a magnificent wooden ceiling with his family emblem of a magpie painted between the beams (*cecca* meaning magpie, a pun on the cardinal's name).

An earlier cardinal's *livrée* (known today as the Petit Palais) had been acquired and enlarged during the papacy of John XXII by one of his nephews, Cardinal Arnaud de Via. Now, following the cardinal's death in 1335, Pope Benedict acquired the palace and proceeded to transform it into the headquarters of the Avignon bishopric. But this was only the preliminary to a far more ambitious project conceived by Benedict, one that was to demonstrate to the wider world that Avignon was now the seat of the spiritual leader of Christendom. He began to build the Palace of the Popes. Significantly he followed the example of Cardinal Ceccano by insisting it be constructed as a bastion—at least on the outside. The site he chose was immediately to the south of the cathedral where a modest building had been established by his predecessor as the seat of the local bishopric. Since it was no longer needed for that purpose with the acquisition of Cardinal de Via's far grander *livrée*, Benedict had it pulled down, along with a number of adjacent houses, in order to make space for the new papal palace. To design it he chose as his architect a man from a town in Languedoc, Mirepoix, where he himself had once been bishop, and who was therefore likely to have been someone he either knew personally or at least had been given good reason to trust.

The architect was Pierre Poisson. A workforce of approximately eight hundred labourers was rapidly assembled, and preparations for the new palace proceeded with remarkable speed. Much of the building material was quarried from the sandstone ridge near Villeneuve and ferried across the Rhône on barges. Stone more suitable for paving slabs was quarried and cut near the town of Caromb, a short distance away in the Comtat. Wood came from the oak forests to the north and west of Avignon and from the pine-covered slopes of the Alps, then floated down-river to the main anchorage below the high rock close to the Pont St.-Bénézet.

Construction work itself began little more than a year after the new pope took office. The first area to be completed was a fortified tower more than one-hundred-and-fifty feet tall. This had a dual purpose: the lower part of the tower came to house the papal treasury including the most important official documents, while the upper floors became the papal apartments. These were essentially modest, as befitted a former Cistercian monk; in fact Benedict insisted on wearing his monk's habit throughout his papacy except on ceremonial occasions. A two-storey chapel was added soon afterwards, followed in rapid succession by four wings which enclosed a large cloister (later a courtyard), each wing being flanked by a protective tower.

By now Poisson had been replaced as architect by another Frenchman, Bernard Candelle. No clear reason for the change has come down to us, but it is not unreasonable to suppose that Poisson may simply not have been up to the job. It was, after all, a massive undertaking far more ambitious than anything he could possibly have designed before. Besides, it was required to be built unusually quickly. Most medieval buildings of this scale and complexity took decades to erect, yet Benedict's Palace of the Popes was all but completed during the seven years of his papacy.

Architecturally the new palace was a hybrid of monastery and fortress. In functional terms it was actually neither of these things, but principally an administrative centre, a place where at last the papal court could operate efficiently after so many nomadic years. In other words the Catholic Church now had an acknowledged headquarters, with its seat of government and its treasury in one single place. And to round off this achievement in 1339 Pope Benedict brought the papal archives to Avignon from Assisi where they had been stored ever since the departure from Italy thirty-four years earlier.

What we know about Benedict himself during his papacy fits uneasily with our impression of the man during his previous years as Inquisitor Fournier. The author of the three-volume Register which had precipitated the downfall of the last Cathars comes across as a fastidious and somewhat unfeeling scourge of bewildered peasants who had innocently found themselves members of a community suddenly labelled "heretical". Fournier's relentless crusade against them has something of a witch-hunt about it. On the other hand it entirely lacked the messianic brutality which had characterized Pope John's hounding of the Franciscan Spirituals. Unlike his predecessor Benedict was not in fact a warlike man. He was a dour and orthodox churchman, by nature a judge rather than an executioner: a man who enjoyed setting the world to rights with a firm hand, but without any touch of cruelty. In modern times he would have made a good commissar, or a prison governor, but never a despot. There was always a certain humility about Benedict, perhaps related to the fact that unlike his predecessors he was neither wealthy, nor a nobleman, but a baker's son (or so it was said) who had done well for himself in this world, yet remained at heart a Cistercian monk, even while occupying the highest office of the Christian church.

But the most striking departure from the practices of his two predecessors at Avignon was his abhorrence of nepotism. Not one of Benedict's nephews was made a cardinal, which must have caused some surprise in a papal Curia which was still heavily weighted with the close relatives of both Clement and John. Benedict's very first act as pope had been to send back to their dioceses all priests who had attached themselves parasitically to the papal court with no adequate reason or invitation. Just as he insisted on retaining the clothing of a Cistercian monk, so he retained a fierce Cistercian sense of moral decorum towards the world he now governed. He cleaned up the place, just as he also strove to clean up a number of religious establishments in the region which had lapsed from the daily disciplines prescribed in the Rule of St. Benedict.

In financial matters he was characteristically cautious. He was fortunate in inheriting from his predecessor a Papal Chamberlain, Gasbert de Laval, who acted as his personal adviser on all financial and administrative matters about which Benedict was largely ignorant and—it was sometimes said—largely incompetent. He also inherited from the miserly Pope John a treasury that was bulging to the point of opulence. This was an inheritance he treated with respect; Benedict was not a man tempted to dispense that bounty on high living or gestures of lavish generosity designed to impress visiting potentates. On the other hand church charities and hospitals regularly benefited from his sense of public duty, as did a number of run-down churches in Rome to which he sent money for much needed structural repairs—perhaps with a twinge of conscience at having reneged on his earlier vow to return the papacy there.

A greater failure, at least in his own eyes, was his powerlessness to curb the conflict between France and England which had been rumbling for many years and finally broke out in the third year of Benedict's papacy in what became known as the Hundred Years War. Papal interest in resolving the conflict between the two countries was principally related to keeping alive hopes of mounting another crusade to the Holy Land. It was perfectly clear to him, as it had been to his predecessors, that so long as the two great military powers of France and England expended their energies and financial resources on fighting one another there could be no possibility of mounting an effective crusade against Islam.

If Avignon failed to play any effective part in the early stages of the Hundred Years War this was largely because in reality the conflict between France and England had virtually nothing to do with the papacy, or indeed with the church in general. It was a matter of hard-bitten politics, a protracted and intermittent tussle between two rival monarchies over their respective claims to French lands and the throne of France itself. And in these overbearing secular issues Benedict found himself powerless to intervene because he was to a great extent irrelevant.

There was to be one real and devastating impact of the Hundred Years War on Avignon, but that was several decades in the future. Meanwhile a conflict of a totally different kind was waiting to break out within the city itself. It was one that would soon be sparked off by a young Italian who was to become among the most celebrated European figures of his day, a man of capacious gifts and intellect which far outreached the narrow horizons of his time, and who was courted by monarchs and churchmen across the breadth of the continent. This was the scholar and poet Francesco Petrarca, more widely known as Petrarch.

§

Petrarch's father had been a friend of Dante in Florence. And like Dante, as a supporter of the Holy Roman Emperor he had been forced to flee the city in 1302 under sentence of death after the pope's party staged a coup and seized power. The family moved to safety in Arezzo, where Petrarch was born two years later. In 1312, attracted by the prosperity of the new papal city, the father moved to Avignon, hoping to find work as a notary among the growing Italian community which had followed the popes there. A year later his wife and two young sons joined him, though for reasons that are not entirely clear Petrarch and his brother were soon dispatched a short distance away from Avignon to live in Carpentras, the capital of the papal Comtat, and where the two boys began their schooling in earnest.

Childhood in Carpentras proved to be a time of great happiness for Petrarch. He loved "the peace in the house, the freedom outside, the silence in the fields, the utter quiet. I thank God for giving me that period of tranquil time," he wrote later. The imprint of the Provençal countryside on the young poet was to prove deep and lasting, nourishing much of his finest lyrical writing in the years to come. Meanwhile at the persuasion of his father law studies followed, first in Montpellier, then back in Italy at Bologna. But he hated studying law, and as soon as his father died Petrarch returned to Avignon and began an ecclesiastical career, at the same time throwing himself into the study of the classical authors, in particular Virgil, who was to remain his inspiration and mentor for the rest of his life. Then, after taking minor orders, he was awarded a post as private chaplain to one of the most powerful figures in the papal court at Avignon, Cardinal Giovanni Colonna, a member of the same Italian family of noblemen who had harassed the unfortunate Pope Boniface at Anagni several decades earlier, indirectly causing the departure of the papacy from Italy.

From this moment onwards Petrarch began to lead a double life. Cardinal Colonna became the young man's patron, and Petrarch the cardinal's protégé, of whom he was justly proud. It was a golden time for the young poet. He was in his twenties, a gilded youth already much admired as a scholar, and who rapidly found himself swept up in the fashionable and glittering social life which had begun to burgeon in Avignon around the papal court. At the same time seeds were being sown in the young man's mind that were soon to grow into a virulent hatred of the place. Petrarch was already beginning to be pulled in an entirely different direction. The years of childhood in the rural Comtat, combined with a deep love of the Latin lyric poets, particularly Virgil, had imbued in him a yearning for the reflective life and peace of the countryside—an existence totally at odds with his present role as a luminary of an opulent papal court.

This growing aversion to court life, combined with a reputation as one of the brilliant young men of his day, led Petrarch to travel widely during the years that followed. He was a tireless letter writer, and quantities of letters survive documenting his journeys to Paris, Florence and Germany, evidently gathering fame and acclaim wherever he went.

Yet the letter which has become an enduring cultural landmark was written much closer to home, in the papal Comtat itself. It was composed in the spring of 1336 when Petrarch was thirty-two, to an Augustinian monk in Paris who was a close friend and his former confessor by the name of Dionigio. The letter begins, quite simply: "Today I climbed the highest mountain in the region." The peak was Mont Ventoux, over 6,000 feet high and situated forty miles north-east of Avignon. There was nothing unusual about having climbed a mountain: shepherds and hunters did it all the time. What was unusual was Petrarch's reason for doing so. His letter continues: "I was moved by no other purpose than a desire to see what the great height was like." With those few plain words Petrarch became the first person on record to have climbed a mountain simply for the experience of getting to the top and admiring the view.

Petrarch explains how in the company of his younger brother he set off from the town of Malaucène, on the north side of Mont Ventoux. He makes no mention of it in his letter, but the route he would have taken passed right by the little rectangular chapel of Nôtre-Dame-du-Groseau where a quarter of a century earlier Pope Clement V would come to pray while staying at the nearby Benedictine monastery as a summer retreat from the blistering heat of Avignon.

It is not hard to follow the route Petrarch took, at least in its early stages. After passing the Groseau chapel the road from Malaucène leads directly to the sheer rock-face of the mountain at a point where the spring venerated by the Celts as a shrine to the god Groselos gushes out between gigantic rocks into a broad lake. From here the modern road, built in the 1930s, zigzags up the steep flank of the mountain. But the old path, the one Petrarch would have taken, veers in a more gentle fashion through the pine-woods to the left, soon becoming a blade of pale limestone that threads its way between massive boulders towards the base of the mountain. The passage of centuries is largely irrelevant in places like this. Paths are timeless: the same tracks have been used summer and winter since the first arrival of man with his animals and his crops. Today, as ever, the silence here in this wilderness is broken only by the wind and the sound of distant sheep bells, and in the spring by a chorus of nightingales amplified by the huge sounding-board of the mountain ahead.

Soon the path becomes faithful to Petrarch in one special way: it shows no sign whatever of actually ascending the mountain, much preferring a meandering and scenic course along the lower slopes. If anything it tends to go down rather than up. The mystery of why Petrarch should have chosen it is solved by the poet's own written account. "We made ready for the ascent and started to climb at a good pace," he writes in the letter to Dionigio.

*But, as often happens, fatigue soon followed our strenuous efforts, and
before long we had to rest upon some rock. Then we started again,
but more slowly, I specially taking the rocky path at a modest pace.
My brother chose the steepest course straight up the ridge, while I took
an easier one which turned along the slope. And when he called out
in order to show me the shorter way I replied that I hoped to find
an easier way up, and that I did not mind taking a longer course if
it were not so steep. But this was merely an excuse for my laziness,
and when the others had already reached a considerable height I was
still wandering in the hollows, and having failed to find an easier
means of ascent I had only lengthened the journey and increased the
difficulty of the climb. Finally I became disgusted with the tedious
way I had chosen, and decided to head straight up. By the time I
reached my brother, who had managed to have a good rest while
waiting for me, I was tired and irritated.*

Petrarch's sentiments have an easy-going contemporary
ring about them Yet very soon we are reminded that this is the
fourteenth century, not the twenty-first, and that Petrarch, besides
being a man of God, was also a man of the Middle Ages who
shared the medieval obsession with symbols. Hence his account
of the ascent of Mont Ventoux develops into a dialectical exercise
concerning the moral significance of this memorable occasion.
For some quite unexplained reason the poet had taken with
him the copy of St. Augustine's *Confessions* which Dionigio (the
recipient of the letter) had recently presented to him. And on
finally reaching the summit of the mountain Petrarch proceeded
to open the precious volume and read appropriate passages aloud
to his brother, who was apparently deeply impressed. Then, after
weighing up the philosopher's thoughts about the human soul,
he delivered a solemn judgment on his own endeavours with the
following truism: "No man's wit can alter the nature of things,
and there is no way to reach the heights by going downwards."

Climbing his mountain seems to have satisfied Petrarch's curiosity: there is no record of his ever being tempted to do it again. Early the following year he visited Rome for the first time, and it was here that he became convinced that the papacy must urgently return to Italy—a burning conviction he never lost. As a result the journey even further intensified his dislike of Avignon. "Having returned," he wrote later in what

he described somewhat grandly as his Letter to Posterity, "I experienced the innate repugnance I have always felt for city life, and especially for that disgusting city of Avignon."

In that same year he decided to escaped the "disgusting city", discovering instead a retreat deep in the Comtat countryside at what is known today as Fontaine de Vaucluse. Here he remained for the next four years writing lengthy epic poems in Latin and drinking in the grandeur and solitude of nature. Vaucluse was Petrarch's *vallis clausa*, his beloved "closed valley", where the River Sorgues gushes out of the mountainside from a depth of more than one thousand feet. One of the natural spectacles of Provence, today witnessed by more than a million-and-a-half visitors every year, was first described by Petrarch nearly seven hundred years ago: "I discovered a very narrow valley, solitary and delightful, called Vaucluse... Near the headwaters of the Sorgues gigantic rocks lift into the sky on either side, where they receive the winds and clouds. Fountains pour out at the base of these rocks... The Sorgues gushes out of a cavern and with a mighty din rolls its sweet and icy waters over a bed carpeted with small pebbles that look like emeralds."

Petrarch's yearning for solitude needs to be taken with a certain pinch of salt. His "guest-list" at Vaucluse included, among other noble visitors, King Robert of Naples, with whom he had stayed while in Italy and who had become a devoted friend and admirer of the poet. Petrarch also endeavoured to persuade his patron, Cardinal Colonna, to join him. "If to the uproar of the city you prefer the quiet of the fields, come and enjoy it here... I promise you a bed under the shade of trees, a concert of nightingales, figs and grapes, water fresh drawn out of the river—in a word, everything that can be had from Nature's hands, the only fountain of true pleasures."

In spite of his declared loathing of Avignon Petrarch had managed to father an illegitimate child there during the same year as his retreat to Vaucluse. He writes sparingly about his domestic life and we do not know whether the mother and son, named Giovanni, regularly joined him for periods in the country. What we do know is that his household in Vaucluse was modest, consisting of one servant and his wife; the latter's appearance he described laconically: "If Helen had looked like her, Troy would be standing now." But if he is guarded about his family arrangements he describes his daily life at Vaucluse with a freshness that would have delighted his Latin mentor Virgil: "I go out with the first light, and whether in the fields or in the house I am busy thinking, reading, writing... Every day I wander on the barren mountains, in the dewy valleys, among the caves; I often pace on either bank of the Sorgues... In the morning I seek the hills, in the evening the meadows."

Then there was the other side of his life. For all his love of solitude and seclusion, such was Petrarch's fame by this time that after three years in Vaucluse he received two letters on the same day, the first an invitation to Paris to receive an official honour for one of his Latin epic poems, the other a letter signed by representatives of the Roman senate inviting him to be awarded the crown of olives as Poet Laureate. Not surprisingly he chose the latter, whereupon he travelled to Rome a second time and was duly crowned on the Capitol Hill on Easter Day, April 1341. It was the highest honour any poet could receive and it meant that he was perceived to be the natural heir of Virgil. Nothing in his long life would have given him more pleasure.

§

One particular association with Avignon coloured Petrarch's feelings about his adopted city in a special and agonizing way, and it lasted until his death. This was his passion for the legendary Laura, a woman as celebrated in the literature of love as Dante's Beatrice and Shakespeare's Dark Lady of the Sonnets, and equally anonymous. From his letters and the 366 poems in Italian inspired by her (the *Canzoniere*) we know an enormous amount about what he felt about her, but virtually nothing about her beyond the beauty of her eyes, which obsessed him. Even her identity is not known for certain and has been much disputed, though the most likely candidate is Laura de Noves, who was already married to a nobleman by the name of Hugues de Sade, a distant ancestor of the notorious Marquis de Sade. All we can be sure of is that Petrarch first caught sight of her leaving a service at the convent Church of St. Claire on Good Friday in the year 1327.

The church itself was wrecked during the French Revolution, and was subsequently sold in plots in the approved anti-clerical fashion of the times. But a plaque set into the wall of 22 Rue du Roi-Réné, now a fairly nondescript back-street of Avignon, identifies both the place and the historic moment. It reads "Here in the 14th century stood a church where Petrarch saw Laura for the first time." How many commemorative plaques across the Western world record a mere meeting of eyes?

Petrarch was then a young man of twenty-three who had just returned from Bologna and given up legal studies in favour of a scholarly life of letters in the papal city. The encounter with Laura that Good Friday was a *coup de foudre*, and for the rest of his life he was to adore her, mostly from afar. Many years later he recorded that first moment on the fly-leaf of his personal copy of Virgil (now in the Ambrosiana Library, Milan): "Laura, remarkable for her own virtues, and long celebrated by my verses, first appeared to me during my youth on April 6th in the year Our Lord 1327, in the Church of St. Claire in Avignon." From the morning of that brief encounter Petrarch proceeded to "enter that labyrinth from which I think there is no way out."

There was certainly no way out for Petrarch; nor for one moment did he wish there to be. Laura remained his obsession and—most of all—his muse. "The little I am," he wrote, "I am because of you." Her unavailability seems to have been an important ingredient of his passion for her. He loved the idea and the ideal of Laura. He even loved her indifference to him, her "tranquil disdain", as he put it. The poetry flowed, and the longing for her refused to die, even after Laura herself died. It all sounds to us remarkably nineteenth-century; Petrarch's romantic sentiments foreshadow with uncanny precision those of Dante Gabriel Rossetti or Alfred de Musset. At the same time they are sentiments which also hark back to the early-medieval troubadour tradition in which true passion was only believed to exist outside the institution of marriage, and unsatisfied longing was placed at the very centre of the poetic concept of love. What mattered most was not fulfilment, but desire. And Petrarch certainly suffered from no lack of that.

For the troubadour poets love was an elaborate courtly game, and there is something of the courtly game about Petrarch's adoration of Laura. Even in her absence he felt that she governed his life. She was the real reason, so he claimed, why he chose to retreat from Avignon to his "closed valley". "In this desperate state I perceived a rock upon a sacred shore, a refuge against disaster. And now, hidden among hills, I weep my past life... In this valley closed about on all sides, pensive and with slow steps, I walk with my love... The wilder the place where I am, the lonelier the shore, the more my thoughts bring her before me."

It is hard to know what to make of all this. It is equally hard to reconcile the love-sick poet wallowing in his loneliness with the tireless worldly traveller who was lionized wherever he went. "The greatest kings of this age have loved and courted me," he commented. "They may know why: I certainly do not." Another myth! Of course Petrarch knew perfectly well, and was rightly proud of it.

Not everyone was taken in by his protestations of helpless love. An old friend from his days in Bologna, Giacomo Colonna (a relative of his patron Cardinal Colonna and now a bishop), wrote to him with unsparing frankness in 1335: "Your Laura is only a ghost built up out of your imagination so that you may have a subject to exercise your Muse with and make a name for yourself... If there is any reality at all in this, it is your passion, not for your fictitious Laura but for that Laurel which is the crown of poets." To which Petrarch replied: "Would to God that my Laura was an imaginary person, and that my passion for her was only a game. Alas, it is a frenzy..."

The one piece of evidence which might have cleared up the mystery of who Laura was, and what she looked like, went missing long ago. This was a portrait of her which Petrarch commissioned from the most celebrated painter ever to work in Avignon. He was the Sienese artist Simone Martini. There are a number of references to the portrait in Petrarch's writings, including two of the *Canzoniere* sonnets in one of which he writes of "il mio Simon". Martini, a fellow-Italian, was clearly a friend of the poet, and it would appear that the portrait was small and painted on a sheet of parchment facing the opening page of a volume of classical texts, mainly of Virgil. The clearest reference to the "missing Laura" is in one of Petrarch's maudlin homilies on the state of the world ("De Contemptu Mundi"), in which he puts into the mouth of St. Augustine the mention of a "likeness" of Laura "by the skilful hand of a famous artist which you have with you hanging on your person everywhere you go, the subject of permanent and continual tears." We know from his ascent of Mont Ventoux that Petrarch had a habit of carrying favourite books around with him; and if he did indeed wear Simone's fragile portrait of Laura round his neck on his extensive travels round Europe then it is hardly surprising that it failed to survive.

Equally tantalizing is that Petrarch also owned a painting by Giotto, likewise no longer surviving. The painter was nearly forty years older than Petrarch, but the two men would certainly have known one another since they both spent a period of time in Naples at the sophisticated court of King Robert, and one imagines that the painting, whatever it was, was acquired directly from Giotto at that time. All we know for certain is that Petrarch left it in his will to the ruler of Padua, the city which already possessed one of Giotto's greatest fresco cycles, on the walls of the Scrovegni Chapel.

It is intriguing to speculate that Giotto might so easily have spent his last creative years in Avignon rather than in Florence. Even more intriguing is to imagine what artistic glories Pope Benedict's new papal palace might have possessed—and still possess to this day. Instead two factors above all prevented any such eventuality. First, Benedict had been a Cistercian monk, and in his heart still remained one, and the Cistercian ethic, inherited from the ascetic St. Bernard of Clairvaux, scorned pictorial imagery as an undesirable distraction from the spiritual life. So, there was never going to be any art commissioned by Pope Benedict. Secondly, the taste of the papal court in general inclined not towards the art of Florence, where Giotto came from, but to that of its rival Tuscan city, Siena. Hence it was not Giotto who came to take advantage of the expanding wealth and patronage of Avignon, but the artist who was to paint the portrait of Laura, Simone Martini.

Simone was a man in his mid-fifties at this time, and he arrived from Siena in the year 1339, or possibly a few years earlier, remaining in the papal city until his death in 1344. For many years he had been unchallenged as the principal painter to the republic of Siena. As a young man he would have witnessed the most celebrated painting of its day, Duccio's enormous *Maestà*, being paraded triumphantly through the streets of the city before being set up behind the high altar of Siena cathedral. In the succeeding decades Simone had become the most successful and prolific painter in all Europe after Giotto, and almost certainly the richest. His prestigious commissions had included frescoes in Siena's cathedral and Palazzo Publico, and a series of frescoes on the life of St. Martin in the lower church of St. Francis at Assisi, a building more famously decorated by Giotto—most of which still exist. He had also executed numerous commissions for paintings in churches throughout Tuscany, and had produced a majestic altarpiece for that most liberal of patrons who had also extended his favours to Giotto, Petrarch and Boccaccio—King Robert of Naples.

So, why should such a man with the world at his feet give it all up in favour of Avignon? The answer can best be found in the prestige and unparalleled wealth which the new papal city now commanded, with a generous proportion of that wealth now lavished on building and decorating new palaces and churches. In fact the new Rome was already becoming richer than the old Rome had ever been. In particular there was the wealth and power held by the many Italian cardinals who had moved there with the papal court. One of these was Cardinal Jacopo Stefaneschi, a man who had earlier commissioned Giotto to design a mosaic for St. Peter's in Rome, and who had now conceived ambitious plans for paintings to decorate the entire narthex, or entrance porch, of Avignon's ancient cathedral.

In all probability it was the offer of a commission from Cardinal Stefaneschi, doubtless a highly lucrative one, which persuaded Simone Martini to come to Avignon. It is also possible that younger artists in Siena were beginning to encroach on his supremacy there. In the event, once in Avignon he undertook to paint the entire cathedral narthex, including a semi-circular tympanum above the main door on the theme of the Virgin with a donor (probably Stefaneschi himself) kneeling to receive her blessing, and a large triangular composition above it depicting Christ in Glory. Elsewhere in the narthex he also painted a scene representing St. George and the Dragon; this achieved sudden fame two hundred years later when the princess being rescued by the saint was believed (on no evidence whatever) to be a portrait of Petrarch's Laura. Like Simone's actual portrait of her this, too, has failed to survive, though the Vatican is said to

possess an extremely poor seventeenth-century drawing which is a copy of Simone's original painting, showing the princess on her knees in supplication before her rescuer—an attitude she certainly never assumed before Petrarch.

In the cathedral narthex today Simone's series of masterpieces is no more than a gallery of ghosts: we can just pick out how the artist first sketched each composition directly on to the bare limestone walls. The design was then copied on to a prepared surface ready for the application of a layer of wet plaster which would receive the paint itself, fixing the colours as it hardened and dried. The result was what we know as fresco, the method of decorating large areas of wall space that was favoured by most Italian church painters of the era. Yet, exposed to the elements as well as the vandalism of revolution and religious wars, Simone's frescoes were subsequently spared no indignity, until after the passage of more than six hundred years what little remained of his paintings was finally removed for safe-keeping to the Papal Palace after the Second World War. In the course of lifting the frescoes from the walls the restorers discovered Simone's full-scale working drawings (in red chalk made from iron oxide and known as *sinopie*) which lay directly beneath the painted plaster; and in 1960 these too were transferred to the Papal Palace where they now grace the walls of the spacious room known as the Consistory, formerly the meeting place and reception hall for visiting ambassadors and legates.

By and large Avignon failed to do justice to the most gifted artist who ever came to work here. Apart from these ghostly relics from the cathedral narthex his years of residence have nothing to show for them. His patron, Cardinal Stefaneschi, died even before the cathedral frescoes were completed, and we have no record of other patrons who may have employed him, whether to paint portraits or create church altarpieces. Certainly he never held any official position at the papal court, or records would have shown it, and there is no sign that he ever painted anything for Benedict's new papal palace. But then the austere Cistercian pope, with his suspicion of religious imagery, would never have wanted to employ the painter whom Bernhard Berenson once described as "the most lovable of all the Italian artists before the Renaissance".

As it transpired, Simone Martini was a generation too old. Had he been twenty years younger and arrived in Avignon in 1344, instead of dying in that year, he would surely have found work in plenty, because soon it was to become dazzlingly clear that Benedict's successor as pope, Clement VI, was everything Benedict was not. He was to become a true prince of extravagance and high living, a man for whom nothing would ever be too splendid for the papal court over which he presided, or for the papal palace he was to transform from fortress to mansion of luxury. Instead of Simone it was to be a later generation of artists from Siena who would reap the rewards that flowed in torrents from the place Petrarch described so contemptuously as "that Babylon".

Meanwhile, on 25 April 1342 Pope Benedict XII died, it was said of gangrene, though Petrarch claimed that he was merely an old man weighed down by age and wine (unlikely for a Cistercian monk, one would have thought, but then Petrarch was rarely given to impartiality). The period of official mourning was long drawn-out even by the standards of the day; the funeral ceremony held in Avignon's cathedral lasted a full nine days, with the pope's catafalque hung with black silk beneath candelabra likewise draped in black. Finally the man who had been the scourge of the last Cathars was allowed to be buried, wearing—as a modest personal touch—his favourite cork slippers. And so Cistercian austerity accompanied him even to his grave, though, alas, the slippers are not evident on his stone effigy in the Gothic tomb which today dominates the side-chapel of the great cathedral.

None of the priests and courtiers who guarded the grim black catafalque through those nine days could possibly have imagined how radically the austere mood of the papal court was shortly to change. At the bidding of Benedict's successor, Clement VI, an avalanche of extravagance and splendour was about to descend on Avignon, until the papal city would very soon outshine all the royal courts of Europe.

As if the popes were still in Avignon: the coat-of-arms of Clement VI gracing the entrance to the papal palace.

6

To Live Like a King

Like those before him the fourth Avignon pope was a Frenchman. He became known as Clement the Magnificent, and he made quite sure he lived up to the title. "My predecessors," he claimed, "did not know how to be pope."

Clement VI most certainly did know how to be pope. For him, being head of the Christian church meant not only ruling it like a king, but living like a king—with sumptuous luxury, profligate self-indulgence, unquestioned authority, a vast entourage of attendant lords and flunkeys, morals that were for the most part tailored to suit himself, and (equally important) an unbounded generosity towards all around him. "A pontiff should make his subjects happy," he assured those who flocked to his papal court in ever-growing numbers to enjoy the favours which the great man showered about him throughout his ten years as Supreme Pontiff. Without actually inheriting a kingdom Pope Clement managed none the less to be the greatest monarch of his day. His papal court became in effect a royal court. And God's throne on earth was the most splendid throne of them all.

Besides all this, Clement was also one of the most talented men of his time. Born Pierre Roger about the year 1291, he came from a family that has been described as "lesser nobility" in the Limousin region of Aquitaine. As a young man he became a Benedictine monk. He also obtained two doctorates in Paris (in theology and canon law), afterwards becoming abbot successively of the monasteries of Fécamp and La Chaise-Dieu before being appointed archbishop of Sens and

Rouen (simultaneously). Soon he was appointed Chancellor and chief minister of France by King Philip VI, to whom he remained a close and devoted friend. He was subsequently created a cardinal by Pope Benedict XII in 1338, just four years before succeeding him as pope. He was by this time a man in his early fifties.

Once again the cardinals had chosen a man radically different from his predecessor. Indeed it would have been hard to find a churchman anywhere in Europe less like the austere Cistercian monk who had occupied the papacy before him. Clement was consecrated as pope in Avignon cathedral on 19 May 1342. At the coronation procession two members of the French royal family—John Duke of Normandy and Eudes Duke of Burgundy—ceremonially led Clement's horse by the bridle, one on either side, an honour normally accorded only to an emperor. A further indication of the way he intended to conduct himself as Supreme Pontiff was the coronation banquet in the Papal Palace which immediately followed the consecration. This was held for no fewer than 3,000 guests, and it was recorded that the following items were prepared for the occasion: 1,023 sheep, 118 cattle, 101 calves, 914 kids, 60 pigs, 10,471 hens, 1,440 geese, 300 pike, 46,856 cheeses and 50,000 tarts. And to wash it all down some 200 casks of wine were delivered for the occasion, all of them duly consumed.

If his immediate predecessor often seemed to possess little or no personality beneath that grey exterior, no one could ever harbour such doubts about Clement. In the context of history he remains one of the most colourful men ever to have occupied the papal throne, as well as one of the cleverest. As a public figure he was judged to be among the finest orators of his day; he relished delivering speeches whenever the occasion presented itself, and he especially enjoyed preaching from the pulpit of Avignon's ancient cathedral. His hospitality was equally famous. It was said that no one ever left his presence empty-handed, particularly the scores of hopeful clerics whom Benedict had taken pains to banish from Avignon, but who now returned in droves seeking lucrative benefices from the new pontiff, which he graciously handed out. There were as many as one hundred thousand benefices offered during the period of his papacy according to one chronicler and eye-witness.

Exaggeration or not, there is no doubt that Avignon under Clement was a haven for careerist churchmen delighted to be able to draw a comfortable income from parishes they rarely visited while they themselves enjoyed the fleshpots of the papal court. Boccaccio's tales of lewd and indolent priests in the pages of *The Decameron* were by no means entirely fictional. The book was written during the period of Clement's pontificate, and although Boccaccio seems never to have visited Avignon he was a close friend of Petrarch who would certainly have taken any opportunity to vilify the papal city whenever the two writers met in Italy.

Clement's celebrated largesse was in fact a great deal more than the actions of a warmly generous spirit: it was also a shrewd instrument of personal authority. Within two years of his election as pope Clement proclaimed unequivocally that "powers of disposal of all churches, dignities, offices and ecclesiastical benefices are vested in the Roman pontiff." In other words, even though now in Avignon the pope was still Bishop of Rome, successor to St. Peter and St. Paul, and therefore God's appointed vicar on earth with the sole authority to appoint whomsoever he wished to serve and govern God's church. He, and he alone, was in charge. It was part of Clement's policy of centralization, of gathering the reins of temporal power firmly into the hands of the papacy, and not surprisingly it caused profound dissatisfaction among bishops right across Europe who saw their traditional powers of appointment taken from them at a stroke. Clement was determined to be the monarch of his church. And monarchs prefer to share power with no one.

At the same time the papal court over which he presided seems to have been a far more easy-going and contented body of churchmen than had gathered round his predecessor, Benedict. Cistercian rigour had been replaced by an altogether more pleasure-loving view of the religious life. Gone, too, was Benedict's strict edict against nepotistic appointments within the church. By contrast Clement's own family and friends found the warmest of welcomes to the new Avignon, no doubt adding considerably to the lustre and jollity of the place. During his ten-year reign as pope he appointed twenty-five new cardinals (twelve of them in a single month in 1350) of whom twenty-one were French, and at least ten of them closely related to him either by blood or by marriage. One of these was his younger brother Hugues Roger, and three others were his nephews including one, Pierre Roger, who was widely rumoured to be his own son, and who twenty years later was to become the last of the seven Avignon popes, Gregory XI. There was also a "niece" who found herself awarded the title of "rectrice" of the papal Comtat, a post which seems to have carried no defined responsibilities.

All in all, Clement's Avignon was becoming increasingly a mirror of a royal court, one that was in fact considerably more opulent than the court surrounding the then king of France, Philip VI. Clement himself had spent many years as a young luminary of that court in Paris, and now, as pope, he remained one of King Philip's most respected advisers, especially on legal matters. This trusting relationship was yet another prop to Clement's position of authority within the Christian world. It is not hard to imagine what his namesake Clement V, the first of the Avignon popes, would have given for such respect from the French monarch he had been compelled to deal with, instead of finding himself little more than the royal puppet.

Whatever the profligacy of Clement's own spending, it was during his ten-year pontificate that Avignon became a city that was enviably wealthy in the eyes of Europe as a whole. From being a small and relatively insignificant town a mere forty years earlier it was growing into one of the great capitals of the world. Some of the richest and most influential people in Europe now chose to live in Avignon, or at least to keep a base there. They included royalty, among them the Prince of Orange and (less surprisingly since she actually owned the city, having inherited it from her grandfather) Queen Joanna of Naples. As for the cardinals, they were men who had acquired some of the most lucrative benefices in the whole of Christendom, and in consequence many of them possessed colossal wealth, as their wills eloquently testify. Cardinal Lagrange left his heirs vineyards and beautifully-kept gardens on the edge of the city as well as a château and several houses at Sorgues, a few miles to the north. Then there was Cardinal Hugues de Reziers de Maunont, one of Pope Clement's brothers, who left nearly 150,000 gold florins as well as gold and silver vessels and a huge quantity of jewels. Other cardinals are known to have kept musicians and troupes of entertainers as regular members of their households, while it was quite normal for a cardinal to own a stable of the finest Arab horses, or a number of trained falcons to satisfy his passion for hunting, or a menagerie in the grounds of his *livrée* which would include a variety of exotic animals including monkeys, lions, bears and even a camel or two.

Everything about the life of the rich contributed to the prevailing cult of *magnificantia*. And since great wealth attracts further wealth it was not long before Avignon became one of the major banking centres of the Christian world, eclipsing all other cities in the region including Marseille, Nîmes and Montpellier. Once established in the city Florentine bankers began to provide a variety of invaluable financial services, changing currencies, transferring money safely from one city to another, arranging loans, providing security for the storage of precious objects. At the same time Avignon was becoming a favourite marketplace for international merchants, many of them Italians, especially Tuscans. Florentine merchant companies satisfied the growing demand for luxury goods, importing silks, gold thread, oriental spices, fine cloth from Flanders, French linen, as well as all manner of *objets d'art*. The River Rhône had never been busier, and the quays alongside the Pont St.-Bénézet were now regularly crammed with vessels loading and unloading precious goods from all parts of the known world to the accompaniment of many languages—chief among them French and the Tuscan dialect of Italian, both mingling with the local Occitan, or *langue d'oc*, the indigenous language of the street and of the region as a whole.

In this respect, as in so many other ways, Avignon was changing rapidly. The original population had been small, a mere five thousand or so. But now numbers were multiplying year by year as the commercial wealth of the city, as well as the prestige of its papal court, was attracting immigration from all over Europe on an ever-increasing scale. The result was a floating population of people from all walks of life, from rich merchants lining up a fortune for themselves to humble petitioners pleading for favours at the papal court; from inquisitive visitors anxious to sample this wonderful new Babylon to poor country people seeking to join the workforce of unskilled labourers who were required to build and service the place. Altogether Avignon was beginning to be overrun by outsiders trying to find ways in which they might belong and thrive there.

As a result it was hardly a safe or settled city. Accommodation was at a premium; people arriving in search of work were often compelled to sleep in the streets, or along the banks of the Rhône, or even in the overcrowded cemeteries. Taverns and inns sprung up in plenty, and duly overflowed. Drunkenness and violence among the numerous rival factions erupted regularly, only fractionally curbed by a curfew imposed at nightfall by the authorities attempting without much success to contain this social cauldron. Prostitution was rife; there are records of at least eleven brothels in one area of the city alone. And inevitably, with such a huge and random influx of people in search of work, there was rarely enough of it to go round, resulting in widespread unemployment, hardship and yet more violence. Pope Clement did his best by expanding the *pignotte* (the charity office for handing out food) which Pope John had instigated, and by contributing a large garden close by where fruit and vegetables could be grown and distributed among the needy.

Physically the city was expanding almost by the day. It had already spread far outside the original ramparts, which in any case had never been adequately reconstructed since Louis VIII had torn them down more then a century earlier as a reprisal for Avignon's tacit support of the Cathars. The area beyond the old walls was now turning into a colossal building site, with ramshackle wooden houses hastily thrown up to accommodate the drifting population. Many of the indigenous inhabitants, too, were compelled to move out into this squalid suburban wilderness, their former homes having been ruthlessly sequestered and torn down by the cardinals or by nobility in order to make way for yet more sumptuous urban mansions.

In fact Avignon was a fine place to live if you were rich. The new wealth of the city was certainly not a commodity distributed evenly among its inhabitants; huge profits for some went alongside considerable poverty and social disruption for many others compelled to live in what must have resembled a hastily assembled refugee camp. As so often, the most eloquent witness to the dark side of Avignon is Petrarch, here in full rhetorical flow: "What words can express how one is nauseated by the rank-smelling alleys, the obscene pigs and snarling dogs, the rumble of wheels shaking the walls, and the carts blocking the twisted streets? So many races of men, so many horrible beggars, such arrogance of the rich! In short, so many ill-fitting human beings of diverse customs, such a clamour of mingling voices, and such a throng of jostling bodies!"

And yet, for those who were able to take advantage of the flood of new wealth life was extremely rosy. Artists, architects, stone masons, craftsmen and artisans of all kinds, anyone who possessed a practical skill, found work in plenty, as did lawyers, scribes, translators, traders, teachers, in fact anyone who could satisfy the requirements of the newly wealthy, or service the needs of an increasingly overweight church bureaucracy.

Amid this discordant mêlée the papal court was becoming vastly swollen in numbers. The legal training of Pope Clement and his predecessors certainly contributed to the growing complexity of church administration, as did Clement's own policy of centralized control of clerical appointments and of church affairs in general. It is estimated that around five hundred papal officials now worked for the papacy in Avignon, and these were supported by at least three times that number of lay staff also on the papal payroll. How many were hangers-on is impossible to establish—probably a fair number given Clement's grandiose generosity.

None the less, parasites and indolent courtiers notwithstanding, the core of the papal court remained the Curia Romana, the administrative body which enabled the pope to govern the church, and for which he was personally responsible. Like any governing body, or civil service, the Curia was made up of a number of self-contained departments. In addition the pope had an informal advisory body around him consisting for the most part of near relatives and trusted friends who acted as a kind of unofficial cabinet, and who were themselves served by numerous attendant officials, stewards, chaplains, secretaries, doctors, chamberlains, librarians and other handy functionaries who could be called upon at any time.

Then there was the Sacred College, made up of the cardinals themselves, whose responsibility it was to elect any new pope, and who were in turn appointed by the pope. Again, each cardinal would be attended by any number of officials, chaplains and secretaries, as well as maintaining his own household of at least twenty, and sometimes as many as fifty, employees, each household resembling a miniature papal court. It is not hard to understand why the locally-born population was finding it increasingly difficult to keep a foothold in the city.

The financial affairs of the church were conducted by the Apostolic Chamber (or Camera), a body of special importance during Clement's spendthrift papacy since it was responsible for collecting taxes from the entire Christian world. The pope's own finances were directed by a Chamberlain who was in effect his Finance Minister, supported by a

Papal Treasurer, numerous clerks, notaries, couriers and quantities of legal staff. The vast amount of correspondence required by the papal administration was the job of the Chancery, staffed by a veritable army of scribes. The more spiritual areas of such correspondence rested in the hands of a Papal Penitentiary, headed by a cardinal with the title of Grand Penitentiary, and whose role included the awarding of dispensations and absolutions as well as handing out certain punishments. There was also a department dealing with legal administration, as well as a Papal Tribunal with a staff of advocates permanently on hand to deal with a wide variety of cases and appeals.

If these bodies represented the administrative core of the Curia, then the papal court also incorporated legions of supplementary staff. There were armed guards in large numbers and a variety of ceremonial officers who helped conduct the numerous formal parades and public functions of which Pope Clement was deeply fond. His own personal armed escort might be accompanied by liveried sergeants-at-arms, porters, grooms and servants of all kinds, and by mounted knights and squires with no identifiable function other than to display themselves in their finery, being men who had chosen to attach themselves decoratively to the papal court as an agreeable way of leading a life of leisure and pleasure.

There was also the palace staff. Here was yet another army, whether in domestic service or engaged in the kitchens, the pantry, buttery, working in the stables or keeping up the palace gardens. Some measure of the size of the papal court may be gleaned from the fact that the kitchens are known to have produced more than three hundred meals in a single typical day, in addition to handing out food for as many as a hundred poor. In fact both the papal court, and the city itself were bursting at the seams. Avignon had already grown larger than Rome.

§

It is hardly surprising that Pope Clement decided to build a larger palace. The gloomy monastic fortress bequeathed by his predecessor was neither large enough for Clement's official needs nor remotely grand enough for his style of living. What he required was a building that could accommodate a hugely-expanded papal bureaucracy, but more particularly one in which he could receive kings as well as live like a king himself. The new palace was therefore one of the very first projects he set in motion—within months of his election as pope. In May 1342 work had already begun. It was designed to abut directly onto Benedict's earlier palace, in effect to be an extension of it on the south side, though on a far grander scale, leaving a spacious quadrangle between the two buildings which was to become the Courtyard of Honour. The new palace was still to be a fortress in appearance, glowering and cumbersome (as it looks to this day), yet behind the bristling turrets and battlements there was a new imagination at work, and some of the finest Gothic architecture of its time was being designed, of a refinement and sophistication which Benedict could never have dreamed of. It was soon to move the contemporary chronicler Jean Froissart to describe the palace as "the most beautiful and strongest house in the world", a phrase which also sums up its dual function. All in all, it was to become the largest private house of its day.

The fresh imagination at work was that of the new architect, Jean de Louvres, who was a Parisian. (Clement, long accustomed to the ways of the royal court of France, was never likely to entrust so prestigious an undertaking to some mere provincial.) The pope wanted only the best. Work certainly proceeded very fast. Within little more than a year the building known as the Wardrobe Tower was completed, along with a further tower devoted entirely to the kitchen, one floor being a larder, a second floor known as the "grape room" for the pressing of fruit, while the entire top floor was given over to a central hearth, complete with a gigantic stone hood open to the sky, and built in such a way as to permit meat to be grilled or spitted on different levels and in suitably huge quantities.

But the enormity of Clement's vision of papal grandeur only became clear once the public rooms were completed during the years that immediately followed. The largest of all the buildings in the new palace was one that was constructed on two levels. On the lower level Jean de Louvres created one of the supreme masterpieces of early-Gothic architecture: this was the Great Audience Hall, designed to house the judicial body known as the Court of Apostolic Causes. The hall is 170 feet long and for weight-bearing purposes was designed to be divided into two naves separated by five elegant pillars on which the ribs of the vaulted ceiling rest. On the level above, approached by a Grand Staircase of Honour, the architect created a second Gothic masterpiece, the Great Chapel. This repeats the dimensions of the hall below, but instead of being divided in two it consists of a single open space made up of seven vaulted bays whose arched ribs merge into columns running like slender threads of stone down the walls on either side. The chapel is lit by tall bay windows each framed by delicate tracery, from one of which—the Indulgence Window in the nearby Loggia— Pope Clement would give his blessing to the crowd assembled in the Courtyard of Honour below.

Other public buildings followed: the Great Promenade, the Grand Dignitaries Wing, the Champeaux Gate, which became the main entrance to the palace (and still bears Clement's coat of arms carved above it), the Great Treasury, the Cloister, the Consistory Hall, where the pope received visiting sovereigns and ambassadors, and the hall known as the Grand Tinel (from the Low Latin meaning "barrel") where he would hold banquets beneath a vaulted roof covered with blue fabric studded with stars to evoke the splendour of heaven (as well as, no doubt, his own splendour). The least public room in the new palace was the Lower Treasury Hall. Here the pope's money and other silver and gold objects were stored in bags hidden beneath the stone slabs of the floor, access to the room being restricted wisely enough to the Chamberlain and the Treasurer, besides the pope himself.

Then there were the two chapels, of St. John and St. Martial, both of them decorated floor to ceiling with frescoes by the Italian artist Matteo Giovanetti, to whom in 1346 Clement awarded the title "painter to the pope". Giovanetti was a native of Viterbo, but his work belongs unmistakeably to the Sienese tradition of narrative painting with a gentle touch of fairytale, as practised here before him by Simone Martini. But whereas Martini had been ignored by Pope Benedict, who as a devout Cistercian wanted nothing to do with the "distraction" of holy imagery, Giovanetti found himself showered with commissions from a pope for whom painting, especially if it contained an abundance of lapis lazuli and gold, was a vehicle perfectly suited to enhance the glory of God and his own high office. As a result Giovanetti remained in Avignon fully employed for the remainder of his working life.

Though much of the new palace is known to be been decorated by Giovanetti, or at least under his direction, his frescoes in the two chapels are the only complete sequences of his work in Avignon to have survived. The commission for the St. John Chapel was for the artist to paint two series, one on the life of John the Baptist and the other on that of John the Evangelist, the former series covering the north and east walls, the latter the south and west walls. Considering the apocalyptic and bloodstained events surrounding the lives of both saints Giovanetti's version of their respective lives is soft, almost playful; but then an absence of solemnity seems to have been a characteristic of his work, and it would most likely have suited Clement's own repugnance for all things austere. Painter and pope were, in this sense, made for one another.

The frescoes in the second chapel had a much closer bearing on the pope's personal interests and in fact take the form of a disguised political statement. The otherwise-obscure St. Martial was a third-century Christian who is reputed to have received instructions directly from St. Peter himself to evangelize the Limousin district of Roman Gaul—which so happened to be where Clement's own family also came from. Accordingly it is easy enough to see how such a link, however putative, between the first bishop of Rome and the present occupant of the papal throne could be interpreted as a justification from the highest possible authority for the papacy continuing to reside in Avignon. Clement was the first of the "exiled" popes not even to have paid lip-service to any intention to return to Rome. France was his country and Avignon his kingdom—and here he had every intention of remaining.

The Palace of the Popes is a giant labyrinth of secrets; walking round it offers a challenge to detect signs of what it might have been like to live there. The eye searches for small clues—or large clues, like the colossal stone fireplaces thirty feet across which testify to the bitterness of the Avignon winter, especially when the ferocious wind, the Mistral, is howling down the Rhône valley from the distant Alps. Or the vast central chimney in the Great Kitchen, in the form of an octagon worthy of a cathedral, allowing the smoke from a hundred spitted suckling pigs to rise into the night sky. Or more modest details, like the broad stone benches beside the windows of the Grand Tinel where cardinals and visiting ambassadors would sit and gaze out over the papal gardens below, with a goblet of perfumed hippocras or warmed Châteauneuf-du-Pape held in hands bejewelled with rings. Or, more modest still, the diamond-shaped earthenware floor tiles glazed in rich greens and blues, turquoise and ochre-red, many of them decorated with delightfully homely motifs of flowers and animals.

These glimpses of everyday life are mirrored in Giovanetti's frescoes supposedly illustrating the lives of saints. It was a particular trait of the artist to intersperse his biblical figures with portraits of men and women who have stepped straight out of the fourteenth-century papal court of Avignon. We can see how they would have dressed, wore their hair, how they would have looked. A contemporary might well have recognized who they were.

But of all the rooms in the palace there are two which offer a particularly vivid glimpse of daily life at the time—or at least of one aspect of it—and they are hidden high up within the Angel Tower and the Wardrobe Tower, and are described as the Pope's Chamber and the Room of the Stag. The first of these, the pope's bedroom, is small—not surprisingly perhaps, though it feels surprising after the vastness of the public rooms. We know from records that in Clement's time the bed itself would have been curtained in crushed velvet and emerald-green taffeta. Today there are just the bare walls. But they are extraordinary walls, covered as if this was a classical Roman villa in a swirling design of branches and leaves evoking the impenetrable density of a forest—one that seems to have no entrance and no exit, not even any discernible shape; yet half-hidden among the entwining foliage are tiny wild birds, lovingly painted, and dotted here and there. It is as though the room were a private aviary, an echo of the real aviaries that the Avignon popes liked to keep; because they all of them loved birds, whether in the wild or caged. It is recorded that Clement VI even kept nightingales, though what is not recorded is whether they could be persuaded to sing for him.

Right next to his bedchamber is one of the most enchanting rooms to have survived from the Middle Ages, or indeed from any age. It has been dubbed the Room of the Stag, and it was in fact the pope's private study, as well as the library where he kept his collection of manuscripts (which included Hebrew works and translations from Arabic as well as Latin classical literature). The dominant feature of the room is the fresco sequence covering every wall, most of it still surviving in spite of the room having been somewhat roughly occupied by soldiers during the nineteenth century. Here, and everywhere we look, we become witnesses to the world of the medieval hunt. The central theme is the stag hunt, but other activities in a huntsman's life are also represented around these walls. Fishermen with their nets gather round a pool. Pale hounds leap through the undergrowth. A falconer strolls among the trees with a bird raised on his wrist. Ferrets pursue rabbits through the thickets. The tree-tops are alive with small birds of all kinds. Around them the branches abound in blossom and wild fruits, while down below children are playing or bathing in a stream. It all has the look of a childlike idyll rather than the scene of blood sports, a celebration of man's delight in the natural world, presented as an enchanted forest in which people go about their daily lives with an air of endearing innocence.

No one knows who painted these scenes, or precisely when. There is a view that they were actually commissioned by Clement's predecessor, Benedict XII, though the colourful quality of these hunting scenes hardly

seems to accord with Benedict's somewhat grey nature. If they date from Clement's reign then it is likely that Giovanetti, as "painter to the pope", would at least have played a supervisory role and perhaps even designed and contributed to them. What matters more than the question of authorship is the fact that Clement should have chosen such a theme as the accompaniment to his place of private study. It is a choice which tells us much that historical records tend to leave out. Chroniclers have generally concerned themselves with the large public matters of the day, ignoring the private man and his private pleasures. The Room of the Stag opens a door on to one key aspect of that private world, making it clear that popes, no less than kings, liked to dream of escaping from affairs of church and state by seeking solace and relaxation in the open countryside and the simple pleasures it offered.

These intensely private paintings in the Papal Palace are a reminder that throughout the Middle Ages the sport of hunting remained among the most favourite of all pastimes for European rulers. Hence, in this most intimate of rooms in the palace, as in so many more flamboyant areas of his life, Pope Clement VI chose to live like a monarch.

A masterpiece of the jeweller's art: the Golden Rose, traditionally a gift from the Avignon popes to the most distinguished visitors to the papal court.

7

Dances of Life and Death

The papal court in Avignon under Clement VI is said to have cost ten times that of the royal court in Paris. And since no French monarch is known to have stinted himself, such an avalanche of papal expenditure almost beggars belief. Even with revenues pouring in from the whole of Christendom the cost of being pope in the style enjoyed by Clement still imposed a colossal burden on the Avignon treasury; by the end of his ten-year papacy the coffers which the parsimonious Benedict had so assiduously filled were all but drained.

Had the Avignon papacy taken place in the eighteenth century rather than the fourteenth there would now be a glittering pictorial record of everything that took place in the papal city during this period of its greatest splendour: the parades, the balls, the lavish ceremonies, the banquets, the extravaganzas of all kinds, the unsparing celebrations in honour of visiting monarchs and ambassadors from every corner of the known world. There would have been a gallery of documentary images matching those of Canaletto's Venice. As it is, the images can only be in the mind's eye: and inevitably these are no more than fragmentary.

Since this was not a secular court (at least not officially so) but an ecclesiastical one, religious functions played a dominant part in the public life of the city and in particular that of the papal court.

There were no fewer than fifty-eight liturgical festivals held every year, in addition to the regular Sunday mass and other services for special occasions such as the visit of royalty or some church dignitary. On all such occasions members of the papal court were required to attend. In fact, liturgical life must have been even more dominant in the papal palace than the lavish and often riotous feasting and debauchery about which so much has been written, not least by the outraged Petrarch. We have precious little precise knowledge of the music that would have been performed on these occasions (*Sur le pont d'Avignon* being the only piece of music popularly associated with the place): none the less the sound of Gregorian chant must have been almost constant, echoing through the hollow galleries of the palace from the Great Chapel, or from the ancient cathedral which stood only a short distance away. (And recordings are available locally of the kind of music which would have been heard in papal Avignon at the time.)

Naturally these religious functions were accompanied by displays of splendour. The Avignon court loved display above almost everything. All liturgical festivals were heralded by sumptuous parades through the streets. In addition every Sunday was marked by a parade or public ceremony of some kind, and so was every occasion on which a foreign prince or monarch was received in the city—and there were a great many of these, its glamour and prestige acting as a universal magnet. Barely forty years after the arrival of the first exiled pope Avignon was already seen as the social as well as the political centre of Christendom, and there was not a ruler in Europe who was not anxious to savour its attractions. Nor were these celebrations confined to members of the papal entourage and visiting celebrities: Pope Clement himself enjoyed taking the morning service at the cathedral of Notre-Dame des Doms, delivering by all accounts memorable sermons, while during Holy Week and on certain feast-days the populus would be welcomed into the Courtyard of Honour of the papal palace where Clement would give his pontifical blessing from the bay window close to Jean de Louvres' Great Chapel, which had just been completed.

Clement's celebrated generosity showed itself in many ways besides his boundless hospitality. On Christmas Day the pope would single out a lord who was thought to have distinguished himself particularly bravely in the service of Christendom by presenting him with a belt of silver, as well as a special sword and a cap ornamented with the finest pearls. The lord so honoured was then required to attend matins where he would read one of the lessons to the congregation. A similar ceremony took place on the fourth Sunday in Lent, when the pope would present to some specially deserving church dignitary a piece of remarkable craftsmanship known as the Golden Rose. And for once we know what it looked like because an example is preserved in the Musée de Cluny in Paris: it was one that was sent early in the fourteenth century to a nobleman and bishop by the very first of the Avignon popes, Clement V. It is a life-size representation of a slender branch of a rose bush delicately wrought in pure gold, with a sapphire set at the centre of the open flower surrounded by several accompanying buds each adorned with pearls and garnets.

The craftsmen who created such ornaments and countless other precious artefacts designed to satisfy the papal taste for luxury, as well as that of his cardinals, were recruited from all over Europe, particularly from France, Italy and Germany. Avignon by now had come to support an international community of artists of all kinds—jewellers, painters, sculptors, master masons—together with leading figures in a host of other professions, among them poets, scholars, doctors, astronomers, theologians, philosophers, and of course entertainers of every description. Collectively they contributed to the reputation of the Avignon court as the most civilized in all Europe. It was a glittering showcase. Life within the newly-built palace and in the *livrées* of the wealthier cardinals seems to have been one unending festival, in many respects more evocative of the Rome of the caesars than the Rome of the popes.

Besides the interminable succession of balls and banquets there were spectacular outdoor events at all times of the year. Jousts and tournaments were held on Barthelasse Island in the Rhône opposite Avignon and linked to it by the Pont St.-Bénézet, which at this time still had its full complement of twenty-two arches and connected the papal city with French territory on the far side of the river beyond the island. Clement, with his insatiable appetite for spectacle, also took special pride in arranging brilliant cavalcades through the streets of the city. Inevitably the pope himself was the central figure in these events, mounted on a white stallion with six nobles accompanying him, a canopy over his head against the summer heat, and an equerry in close attendance to help him mount and dismount.

Eye-witness accounts of these public events are few and far between, but those that have survived paint an elaborate picture of a life of luxury and unmitigated excess, particularly gastronomic excess. Among the most extreme of such sybaritic occasions was a reception given to Pope Clement soon after his election by that expansive churchman whose vast *livrée* was described in Chapter Five, Cardinal Annibale di Ceccano. An Italian who was present has left us this detailed account of the event, with special emphasis on the cost of it all.

> *The pope was led into a room hung from floor to ceiling with tapestries of a great richness. The floor was covered with a velvet carpet. The state bed was hung with the finest crimson velvet, lined with white ermine, and covered with cloths of gold and silver. At dinner four knights and twelve squires of the pope's household waited at table; each of the knights received from the host [viz Cardinal di Ceccano] a rich belt of silver and a purse worth twenty-five gold florins; and the squires a belt and a purse to the value of twelve florins. Fifty squires from the cardinal's suite assisted the papal*

*knights and squires. The meal itself consisted of nine courses, each
containing three dishes, that is a total of twenty-seven dishes. We saw
brought in, among other things, a sort of huge castle which was found
to contain a stag, as well as a boar, several kids, as well as hares and
rabbits. At the end of the fourth course the cardinal presented the
pope with a white charger worth four hundred florins and two rings
valued at one hundred and fifty florins, one set with an enormous
sapphire and the other with an equally large topaz... After the fifth
course they brought in a fountain that was surmounted by a tree and
a pillar, from which flowed five varieties of wine. The margins of the
fountain were decorated with peacocks, pheasants, partridges, cranes
and other birds. In the interval between the seventh and eighth course
there was a tournament, which took place in the banqueting hall
itself. Then a concert brought the main part of the feast to a close. At
dessert two trees were brought in; one of them appeared to be made
entirely of silver, and bore apples, pears, figs, peaches and grapes
of gold; the other tree was as green as a laurel, and decorated with
crystallized fruits of many colours.*

Reading such an account it becomes hard to grasp the reality of
an occasion of this kind. What would it have been like to have
attended it, and how would people have behaved? Historians
have managed to unearth a few curious and revealing details
relating to the eating habits of the pope, such as the fact that
Clement apparently used forks, which at the time were still largely
unknown. These were gold forks for the papal roast, but crystal
ones when the dessert consisted of strawberries, metal being
thought detrimental to the delicate taste of fruit. Other utensils
used regularly were likewise made of gold or silver—goblets and
other kinds of drinking vessel, ewers, sauce-boats, flagons, jugs for
wine, while knives as well as special forks might have handles of
ivory or sometimes jasper.

All kinds of other materials also incorporated threads of gold;
it is recorded that in the year 1347 Clement arranged to purchase
forty lengths of cloth-of-gold from Damascus at a cost of 1,728

florins. (Evidently trading with Islam caused him no qualms even
though he had recently mounted a successful naval assault on
Smyrna, in neighbouring Turkey.) Otherwise his purchases were
well spread across the continent: silks from Tuscany (doubtless
employing the services of those energetic Florentine bankers),
white woollen cloth from Carcassonne, broad cloth from Flanders,
fine linen from Paris or from Reims. As for furs, they came from
wherever enough ermines could be found; and Clement's need for
them was considerable—he is known to have received over one
thousand ermine pelts for his personal clothing, though whether
this represented a single order or an accumulation of many orders
over a period of years is not recorded. In either case it hardly
suggests a hairshirt existence.

Luxury was far from being confined to the pope himself, or to
his cardinals. Ambassadors from every nation in Christendom were
treated in a manner designed to send them back to their masters
with wondrous tales of papal largesse. What was more, the papal
taste for excess was often matched by visiting rulers determined
not to be outdone by their host. England's Duke of Lancaster
arrived in Avignon and remained in the city for six long weeks.
And during that time he kept open house for any members of the
papal court who chose to dine with him. The citizens of Avignon,
it is said, were so impressed by the sight of several hundred barrels
of fine wine being brought to the visitor's lodgings that they
pronounced the duke as having "no equal in all the world".

At the centre of this extravagant *tableau vivant* was invariably
the larger-than-life figure of Pope Clement himself—genial,
charming, generous and spendthrift in the extreme, undisguisedly
vain and self-indulgent, but never (or so it would appear) arrogant
or cruel: a man we can only evaluate by what was said of him
and by looking at the world he created around him—because
we do not even know what he looked like. The carved reclining
figure on the pope's tomb in the abbey church of Chaise-Dieu

(where he was once abbot) is too piously formal to provide useful clues. Apart from a few putative representations in illuminated manuscripts the only known painted portraits were executed many centuries later, and inevitably these are invented images based, if on anything at all, on mere fragments of information, on reports of his character, and on the reputation of the man which long survived him. They are like identikit portraits; and perhaps they should merit our attention for the same reason, because they record fleeting impressions of the man which somehow survived, or at least how tradition imagined him to have been. The best of them hangs in Avignon's cathedral: it shows a bald-headed figure, very composed, with a heavy-lidded searching gaze, and an air of restrained sensuality. He looks likeable, quietly ruthless, and highly intelligent—three qualities which probably sum up as accurately as we can manage the character of the greatest of the Avignon popes.

We may know little or nothing about what people looked like at the papal court, but we do know a good deal about what they wore. The pope's private study, the Room of the Stag, opens a broad window on to their world of leisure, showing how men dressed when they went hunting in the forest, or fishing. In addition to the stylized biblical figures in the chapels of St. John and St. Martial, Giovanetti's frescoes also supply further evidence of the daily costume of both men and women around the papal court. But there are also written accounts, not least from Petrarch. Fashions changed frequently, as nowadays and as always, the length of gowns varying from year to year: "gowns now hide the feet, now reveal our shameful parts," the poet sneered, "sleeves that now sweep the ground, now pinion the elbow, belts that now confine the breast, now hang down below the belly."

Those lower down the social scale obviously had little concern with the changing fashions of the papal court. Men generally wore breeches with a knee-length blouse or jerkin over the top (like the huntsmen in the Room of the Stag), and on their feet coarse leather boots, or else clogs. Every man carried a knife of some description slung on a cord round the waist, and which served a multiple purpose as a working tool, an instrument for cutting up food, and of course as a defensive weapon.

Women's dress was more contentious, at least when in public. Safely at home there was no problem: a woman wore a simple woollen or linen dress, or perhaps cotton if this could be afforded. But on public occasions it could be a very different story, especially among wives and daughters who formed part of the papal court. As such they were expected to contribute to the glitter of Avignon's famed social life, and they appear to have done so in provocative style, often to the discomfort of those who held that a woman's place was in the kitchen or a nunnery. Women's party dresses were often particularly magnificent, brilliantly colourful and adorned with furs during the winter months and with jewels all the year round. Hats were not in fashion, hair being worn loose under a silk veil or bandeau if the woman was unmarried, then afterwards raised in a becoming chignon. The dresses themselves were cut extremely low at this time, so much so that preachers were known to refer to them as "windows of hell".

Altogether the papal palace of Avignon had the air of a hedonistic secular court rather than the celibate capital of Christendom. Clement's own morals seem to have been dubious, to say the least. Rumours abounded, particularly over his relationship with his niece by marriage, the beautiful Cécile, Countess of Turenne, whose sister was married to Clement's nephew and who regularly acted as social hostess at the papal palace, as well as presiding over jousts, tournaments and hunting expeditions. Malicious voices claimed that her regular visits to Clement in the Room of the Stag had little to do with discussing wild game. Petrarch described the countess as "dazzling the crowd with her clever eyes" while shamelessly offering "her incestuous embraces"—presumably to the pope himself, even though she was only his niece by marriage.

It is hard to know how seriously to take Petrarch on the excesses of papal Avignon. As an Italian who longed for the papacy to return to Rome he was blatantly prejudiced about everything to do with "dismal Avignon on its horrible rock". He was never one to mince his words, or to refrain from embellishing a theme if his imagination took flight. "What ignominy to see these people raising magnificent palaces resplendent with gold, and with superb towers which threaten the skies in this new Babylon, while the capital of the world lies in ruins." At the same time there was often a streak of hypocrisy in Petrarch's dealings with the papal court: he was perfectly happy to beg favours from the pope when it suited him. Clement not only agreed to legitimize his son and daughter, but also obtained for the fourteen-year-old boy Giovanni the sinecure of a canonry in Verona cathedral. The pope's generosity towards Petrarch was in marked contrast to Petrarch's contemptuous treatment of the pontiff.

Petrarch's main line of attack against Avignon related to the sexual practices supposedly enjoyed by members of the papal court, cardinals and the pope himself included. Whether it was true that banquets at the palace and in the various *livrées* frequently developed into orgies, we shall never know for certain. Petrarch certainly believed as much, and said so with his customary lack of restraint. ("Prostitutes swarm on the papal beds," he fumed.) Given the strength of his prejudice against everything to do with the city it is probably wise not to take his damning judgments too literally. All the same he was by no means alone in commenting on the moral laxity of Clement's papal court in general, and certainly not alone in describing the pope's' own private morals as "notorious".

The nub of his assault rests in a collection of nineteen letters entitled *Epistolae sine nomine* ("Nameless letters"), only one of which appears to have been actually sent (to a close friend who was a bishop), the remainder being for the most part exercises in high-flown rhetorical fury. Justified or not, they remain among the most vicious condemnations of church morality ever uttered. Here are a few choice examples:

> *I will not speak of adultery, seduction, rape, incest; these are only the prelude to their orgies. I will not count the number of wives stolen or young girls deflowered. I will not tell of the means employed to force into silence the outraged husbands and fathers, nor of the dastardliness of those who sell their womenfolk for gold.*

> *We are devoured by a secret ill: it is not life they are taking from us, it is goodness; we can neither live in virtue nor die with honour.*

> *I know from my experience that there is no piety here, no charity, no faith, no respect, no fear of God, nothing holy, nothing just, nothing fair, nothing sacred, in short nothing human. Friendship, modesty, decency, candour are all banished from here.*

In short it was a place "from which no one has come away better... and thousands have come away worse."

Petrarch chose to be absent from the Avignon he hated during the year when the worst disaster in its history struck the city. The pope he vilified, on the other hand, remained in his palace virtually throughout. The disaster in question was the first major manifestation of the bubonic plague in Europe, known to us as the Black Death.

§

In October 1347 a vessel sailing from a Genoese trading outpost in the Crimea arrived at the Sicilian port of Messina manned by a crew that was sick and dying. Fearful of infection, the local authorities refused permission for anyone to disembark.

However, the black rats on board had other ideas, and swam ashore. Within a short time half the inhabitants of Messina were dead. Within three months the plague had spread throughout the Italian peninsula. Within three years it had penetrated almost every corner of the European continent, extending as far distant as Iceland and Greenland. Altogether an estimated forty million people died—roughly half the population of Europe. It was the worst natural catastrophe in the history of Christendom. The civilization and economy of an entire continent were paralyzed. It felt as if the world itself was dying.

In Avignon the Black Death struck in January 1348, just three months after the fatal vessel from the Crimea had docked at Messina. Within the first few days of the outbreak nearly two thousand people were already dead. It has been estimated that by the autumn of that same year the plague had claimed the lives of up to three-quarters of the population of the city and the surrounding Comtat—as many as 50,000 men, women and children in the city alone. Cardinals and other members of the papal court were struck down just as severely. At a stroke the glamour and glitter of the capital of Christendom had been swept away, and suddenly Avignon was living under the shadow of death.

There are a number of surviving eye-witness accounts of the Black Death, and they make gruesome reading. One of the most chilling is a description of events not in Avignon, but in Florence, a city of much the same size at that time and which suffered in precisely the same way. It was written in that very first year of the plague, 1348, by none other than Boccaccio, and it forms part of the introduction to his satirical masterpiece, *The Decameron*.

> *As the year turned to spring, the plague began quite prodigiously to display its harrowing effects... Its first sign here in both men and women was a swelling in the groin or beneath the armpit, growing sometimes in the shape of a simple apple, sometimes in that of an egg,*

more or less; a bubo was the name commonly given to such a swelling.
Before long this deadly bubo would begin to spread indifferently
from these points to appear all over the body; the symptoms would
develop into dark or livid patches that many people found appearing
on the arms or thighs or elsewhere... No physician's prescriptions, no
medicine, seemed of the slightest benefit.

Boccaccio describes how people reacted in very different ways to the danger of catching the disease. "Some would form into a group and withdraw on their own to closet themselves in a house free of all plague victims; here they would enjoy the good life, partaking of the daintiest fare and the choicest of wines—but all in the strictest moderation, and shunning all debauchery... Others found the contrary view more enticing, that the surest remedy for a disease of this order was to drink their fill, have a good time, sing to their hearts' content, live it up, give free rein to their appetites, and make light of all that was going on... Day and night would find them in one tavern or another, soaking up the drink like sponges, and carousing all the more in other people's houses the moment word got out that here was where the fun was to be had. This was easy enough to do as everyone had let his property go, just as he had let himself go, as if there was to be no tomorrow." And indeed, for most of them there was no tomorrow.

Boccaccio's most chilling observations were of the total breakdown of social loyalties which the epidemic brought about. "One citizen avoided the next; there was scarcely a man who would take care of his neighbour; kinsmen would seldom if ever call on each other, and even then they would keep their distance. But this was not all: men and women alike were possessed with such a visceral terror of this scourge that a man would desert his own brother, uncle would forsake his nephew, sister her brother, and often a wife her husband." And when death came: "Many there were who passed away in the street, by day or by night, while scores of those who died indoors only made their neighbours aware of their death by the stench of their decomposing corpses: the whole city was full of these, and of those who were dying all over the place... Enormous pits were dug in the graveyards once saturation point had been reached, and the new arrivals were dropped into these by the hundred; they were packed in layers the way goods are stored in a ship's hold."

In the papal city itself the fullest account of the Black Death was written by a canon by the name of Louis Sanctus of Beeringen, who was close friend of Petrarch and who happened to be visiting Avignon in the retinue of one of the cardinals at the time of the outbreak. In a letter to friends in his native Bruges he described how more than seven thousand houses in the city were now empty and closed up, with more than half the population already dead. "The suburbs hardly contain any people at all. A field near Our Lady of Miracles has been bought by the Pope and consecrated as a cemetery. In this, since the 13th of March eleven thousand corpses have been buried... Nor must I be silent about the neighbouring area, for at Marseille all the gates of the city with the exception of two small one are now closed, for three-quarters of the inhabitants are dead."

Marseille, like all ports, was particularly vulnerable since it was from ships that the black rats swam ashore, the fleas parasitic on them being the actual carriers of the disease. None of this of course was known at the time: Marseille's locked gates impeded not a single flea. Meanwhile ships laded with merchandise floated unanchored around the harbour, their crews all having died. In addition to ghost-ships there was also a nearby ghost-monastery, in which all the monks were dead except one man, who continued to ring the chapel bell until one day the bell fell silent, because he too had died.

In Avignon and the surrounding area, the canon went on, "it is said that altogether in three months 62,000 bodies have been buried here. The Pope, however, about the middle of March, and

The year 1348: "As the year turned to spring, the plague began quite prodigiously to display its harrowing effects." (Boccaccio, The Decameron).

after mature deliberation, gave absolution till Easter to all those who, having confessed and being contrite, should happen to die of the sickness. He likewise ordered devout processions, singing the Litanies, to be made on certain days each week, and to these events, it is said, people sometimes gather from all the neighbouring districts to the number of up to two thousand; among them many of both sexes are barefoot, some are in sackcloth, some with ashes, walking with tears and tearing their hair, and beating themselves with scourges even to the drawing of blood."

It was a widely held conviction that the Black Death was a judgment of God: that it was His visitation on a sinful world. This mood was to grow angrier once the worst of the epidemic had passed, and the exhausted survivors could begin to put their lives together; it was then that the church itself became seen by many to be the body whose sins had invited the wrath of the Almighty.

But as long as the plague raged there was little time for anger. One man who was at the very centre of the disaster throughout the year-long epidemic was the pope's own physician, Guy de Chauliac. Amidst the host of quack remedies being offered by other so-called doctors—such as bottled wind, unicorn's horn, goats' urine, and a variety of magical amulets—Chauliac chose to perform surgical operations on plague sufferers, cutting buboes open and burning them out with hot tongs, a drastic and hideously painful procedure which he none the less claimed was frequently successful. For a great many whom he visited, though, with "abscesses and carbuncles chiefly in the armpit in the groin", as he recorded, generally "they died in five days." It was Chauliac who recommended to Pope Clement that he seat himself between two huge fires, even in high summer, the heat of the flames no doubt being thought to purify the air in the papal palace. With or without Chauliac's counsel, the pope is also reputed to have worn an emerald ring which when turned to the east was believed to reduce the chances of infection, and when turned to the south to nullify the effects of poison—a reminder that medical science and magic were often indistinguishable from one another.

For month after month a pall of dread hung over the city. Everywhere there was a chilling silence except for the cries of the dying and the creak of carts bearing the dead to their common graves. Among those still alive fear, superstition and folklore created a confusion of desperate remedies. Some people trusted in prayer, some in violent self-punishment, others burnt incense or juniper branches, or trusted in a variety of herbal preventatives such as wormwood, mint, lavender, laurel leaves and saltpetre. Physical contact was avoided as far as possible. In church services during holy communion the host would be offered by the priest on the end of a wooden pole. When required to give extreme unction to a plague victim dying in his house, the priest would apply the consecrated oil to a wad of material fastened to a rod which was then inserted in a "plague hole" cut in the door in such a way that it could touch the victim's face.

Pope Clement did what he could. He placed doctors in different quarters of the city. He engaged carters to transport the dead, and gravediggers to bury them. As Canon Sanctus reported in his letter, Clement purchased a large cemetery in which eleven thousand were buried between mid-March and the end of April. Soon, though, even here there was not enough space, and bodies came to be buried one above the other in graves so shallow that scavenging pigs were seen rooting them out. By the end of the year unburied corpses were littering the streets throughout the city, there being few people left to remove them. Often bodies ended up being heaved into a common pit, sometimes, it was said, still alive; alternatively they were simply tossed into the Rhône, as a result of which the pope resorted to consecrating the river so that those thrown into it would not go to their watery grave unblessed.

Finally as Christmas approached, an exhausted population, or what remained of it, began to realize that the power of the Black

Death was at last on the wane; and on 20 December a column of fire was observed rising above the papal palace. If this was seen as a message of hope from heaven, it had come a great deal too late.

§

The plague has left a varied imprint on the city and on the Comtat generally. In Avignon itself there was a surge of new building in the decade following the year of the Black Death. Many of the old houses left empty after the demise of their owners were now pulled down and replaced by more spacious mansions for those wealthier citizens who had managed to survive the holocaust. With the population now halved, by a piece of chilling irony the once-overcrowded city was suddenly overcrowded no longer, and there was a fresh opportunity to build and to expand. Narrow medieval streets became widened, older buildings refurbished, and parish churches throughout the city greatly expanded.

In the towns and villages around Avignon the imprint of the plague is often a darker one. To this day a number of settlements in Provence and Languedoc still bear the name Malemort. Opinions differ as to whether these places were once plague-pits, mass burial-grounds, or were merely deemed to be unhealthy places to live because the local water was considered impure. Malemort-du-Comtat is one such small town within the papal county, a short distance from the hill village of Venasque which gave the district its name, the Comtat Venaissin. Here in Malemort the historical connection with the plague is echoed by the name of the small square beside the gate in what would have been the town's ramparts, still called the Place des Pénitents. There were a number of religious orders of penitents in Avignon and the papal county, and their adherents increased greatly in number in the aftermath of the Black Death as a beleaguered population sought to see the punitive hand of God directing their sufferings, and to make due penance for their supposed sins.

The year 1348 signalled the first onslaught of the plague in the papal territories. But it was not the last. Two further outbreaks occurred during the remaining thirty years of the Avignon papacy—in 1361, then in 1368, each time killing between ten and twenty per cent of the already devastated population. In fact by the end of the century the population of the whole of Europe was barely half what it had been fifty years earlier. And so these waves of destruction continued, approximately every five years throughout the remainder of the Middle Ages, and intermittently thereafter right up to the eighteenth century.

Evidence that the menace of the plague continued to dominate people's lives more than three and a half centuries after it first struck Avignon survives in the form of a strange construction in the range of hills known as the Plateau de Vaucluse, south of Venasque. This is the remains of a limestone wall, originally five feet in height, which once ran along the crest of the plateau a little to the north of the River Durance, marking the boundary separating the papal Comtat from the rest of Provence to the south. Stretches of the wall are still clearly visible threading their way through pine-woods and across the scrubby uplands through carpets of thyme and wild lavender. Much of the stone has long been reduced to a line of rubble by centuries of ferocious winds and the scrambling of goats, though one section at least has been rebuilt and made a tourist attraction with accompanying maps, historical information and a large notice-board announcing Mur de la Peste—the Plague Wall.

It was built in 1721 by order of the papal vice-legates who continued to administer the Comtat long after the popes themselves had returned to Rome. Each individual commune in this border area was held responsible for constructing its section of the wall, as well as manning it with guards stationed in specially-built stone enclaves, many of which are still identifiable. The outbreak of the plague in that year is known to have been a particularly virulent one. The prevailing view by this time was that the pestilence was transmitted, not by foul air, poisoned water or by the punitive hand of God, but by physical human contact: hence the laborious construction of a wall designed to combat it by sealing off the Comtat from all intruders. The siege mentality which prompted such a decision speaks of nothing less than panic; none the less it was (correctly) held to be true that the plague was brought by sea, and the prevailing fear was that the great ports of Marseille and Toulon were the main culprits. Hence, if people could be prevented from entering the papal territory from those ports by means of a wall patrolled  by sentries then the spread of the disease could be halted.

What the well-meaning authorities did not know was that the plague was transmitted, not by physical contact between human beings, but by fleas—and fleas can hop. The plague wall was only a little more effective than the magic potions that had been prescribed by Pope Clement's physicians four centuries earlier.

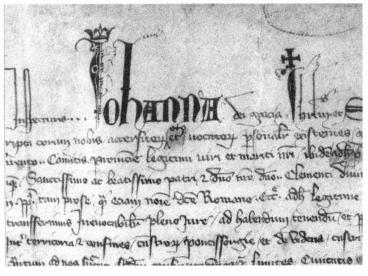

The Bill of Sale: in 1348, at the height of the Black Death in Avignon, Queen Joanna of Naples sold the city to Pope Clement VI.

8

Cross-Currents

In the wake of the Black Death came the backlash of blame. As in every European city the mood in Avignon was dark. People were exhausted, grieving, frightened, and in many cases angry. Why had it happened? There was little understanding of natural causes in the Middle Ages; every occurrence in nature—a drought, an eclipse, an earthquake, a flood—was held to possess some judgmental meaning. Hence a disaster of this magnitude had to be the fault of someone, or of some institution; God would not otherwise have inflicted such dire punishment on mankind. Who was to blame?

The church, traditionally so obsessed with the world's sins, now found itself tarred with its own brush. What could be more blatantly sinful than a papal court that was bloated with wealth and given over to all manner of delights of the flesh? Had not Dante raged against Avignon in *The Divine Comedy*? As for Petrarch, that celebrated voice of wisdom, he had already publicly denounced the place as "the new Babylon".

It began to seem to many survivors of the pestilence that both Dante and Petrarch had been right.

Among those angry people the most extreme were the flagellants, and in a dark foreshadowing of Martin Luther's Protestant Reformation two centuries later the flagellant movement originated in Germany. They consisted of bands of itinerant penitents, many of whom descended on Avignon gathering other disaffected souls along the way. Once here they began to process slowly through the city, barefoot, wearing grey felt hats pulled down over their eyes like hoods, and loose black cloaks slung round their shoulders. Each of them carried a "scourge": this was a whip with three tails of rope knotted at the ends with iron spikes protruding from them. Wailing and shuffling through the streets and into the churches, the flagellants whipped themselves and each other as they went, their cloaks by now saturated with blood.

This was not the kind of aftermath of the plague that Pope Clement would have had in mind. Himself a survivor of the Black Death, and a man who had witnessed the destruction of Avignon's population by as much as two-thirds, he was in no mood to tolerate this latest invasion of his beleaguered city. He roundly condemned the flagellants, threatening them with prison, even with the stake, and promptly issuing two papal bulls against them, the second of which listed one of their grievous crimes as being persecutors of the Jews. They chose to justify this persecution, he claimed, "under the pretence of piety". Clement had already anticipated this outbreak of anti-semitic behaviour; in the summer of 1348, at the height of the plague epidemic, he had issued two further bulls asserting the innocence of the Jews and forbidding all victimization of them on pain of excommunication

By this stance in supporting the Jews Clement set himself squarely against the prevailing anti-semitism of the times. And it stands as the bravest and noblest of all his acts as pope. The fourteenth century in Europe was the era of the most ruthless persecution of Jews until the rise of Nazi Germany six hundred years later. It had begun early in the century when King Philip the Fair of France, forever desperate for money, ruthlessly expelled all Jews from France, seizing their financial assets and their property. Following Philip's death they were readmitted nine years later by royal charter, only to be expelled again in 1322 on the grounds that they had been responsible for poisoning wells, this time their banishment lasting almost forty years. By this time there had grown up a prevailing conviction throughout much of Christendom that Jews simply had no place in a Christian society, and priests everywhere took pleasure in preaching as much from the pulpit to ignorant and credulous congregations.

Among the numerous charges regularly levelled against the Jews the most common was that of usury, lending money with interest, which the Bible denounced as a sin, even though for many centuries Christian leaders had been perfectly happy to take advantage of the financial service that Jews offered.

But it was the Black Death which supplied the sharpest weapons for attacking the Jews. It was widely preached and put about that they had been the prime cause of the pestilence, both by deliberately poisoning wells (yet again) and by practising sorcery or casting evil spells. There was no lack of witnesses eager to offer lurid evidence of the above crimes, and in no time the Jews had become the perfect scapegoat for all the current miseries of the Christian world. Right across Europe tens of thousands were rounded up and either slaughtered on the spot or put to the stake. It is estimated that at least three hundred Jewish communities within the Holy Roman Empire alone were annihilated at this time. Many Jews fled, but it was hard to find anywhere safe to flee to. Hence for those who could make it this far, Avignon and the papal Comtat became the promised land, and Clement VI the first pope in history to be the active saviour of the Jewish people.

It is estimated that a community of at least two hundred Jewish families took advantage of papal protection to settle permanently in Avignon at this time. A great many more made their homes within the boundaries of the papal county, particularly in the capital of the Comtat, Carpentras. At this time Carpentras was a quiet provincial city which had been much loved by Petrarch, who had spent his youth there. Now with the impact of Jewish immigration it began to expand into a flourishing small metropolis. Within a further twenty years Carpentras was to have its own handsome synagogue, surviving to this day as the oldest in France.

The welcome which Clement extended to the Jews in Avignon and the Comtat was unquestionably a brave gesture in the face of such universal Christian bigotry. At the same time it has to be said that the pope's generosity embraced more than a little self-interest. Clement, forever the pragmatist, was an intelligent and shrewd politician, and in opening the city gates to the Jews he showed that he recognized the immensely valuable contribution which the more skilled among the fugitives could make to the papal city, particularly at this time when Avignon was striving to restore its pride and glory after the devastation of the Black Death. A great many of those two hundred resident Jewish families soon became actively engaged in industry and local business, in this way assisting in the rebuilding of a city which was once more rapidly expanding, both in population and in wealth. Clement himself offered a refreshingly straightforward reason for protecting the Jews, namely that Christ had been one. A further indication of the pope's attitude of mind is that a Jewish astronomer known as Leo Judaeus dedicated two of his own works to Clement personally; the pope then had them both of them translated from Hebrew into Latin. A further bonus for Clement was the contribution being made by Jewish doctors. As in Muslim Spain, and in the recently reconquered areas of the Iberian Peninsula, it was Jewish scientists and scholars who were providing access to Islamic studies in such subjects as mathematics, astronomy and, above all, medicine. Jewish doctors who settled in Avignon and Carpentras were invaluable precisely because they understood Arabic, the language being close enough to their own native tongue. Just as without a twinge of conscience Clement could happily trade with Damascus if the finest cloth-of-gold was to be found there and nowhere else, so he saw no problem whatsoever in offering privileges to members of the Jewish faith if their presence could enhance and enrich his city.

§

A document displayed behind safety glass in the Consistory Hall of the papal palace bears witness to one of the most dramatic events to take place in Avignon during Clement's ten-year papacy. It is a bill of sale. And what was sold was Avignon itself.

In fact it is a facsimile: the original—along with other relevant documents—is secreted away in the departmental archives. But it is appropriate that the facsimile should be displayed in the Consistory Hall since it was here that Pope Clement was in the habit of receiving royal and other distinguished guests. And in the early summer of 1348, the summer of the Black Death, the royal guest he received was a young woman of twenty-two who was described by one chronicler of the day as the most beautiful queen who ever lived, and whose reputation throughout Europe was already that of *la douce reine.*

She was Queen Joanna of Naples. She had also inherited the title of Countess of Provence, and it was in this capacity that she was the legitimate owner of Avignon. Here was a further reason—apart from her royal status and her beauty—why Clement should have welcomed her with special warmth and attention. She was in effect his "landlady".

Joanna had fled to Avignon for two closely-connected reasons. Her native city of Naples had been overrun by a murderous body of troops ordered there by King Louis of Hungary, whose brother Andrew had been the husband of Queen Joanna, but who had recently been murdered. Louis was now publicly accusing Joanna of being responsible for the murder: hence the invasion of Naples in support of his dead brother and to assert his own claim to the kingdom of Naples in his place. Joanna's flight to Avignon was therefore to seek protection from her outraged brother-in-law, but more specially to beg for the support of the only man in Christendom with the authority to pronounce her to be innocent of her husband's murder—Pope Clement.

Joanna duly arrived in Avignon early that summer accompanied by her second husband also called Louis—Louis of Taranto. An eye-witness on that day recorded that the queen entered the city on a white horse caparisoned in purple and gold, Joanna herself proudly bearing an orb and sceptre and dressed in a crimson velvet robe over a purple mantle embroidered with gold *fleur-de-lys* and bordered with ermine. (The *fleur de lys* signified that Joanna was actually French, descended from the counts of Anjou, cousins to the French royal family.) Attendant noblemen acting as bearers rode beside her holding a gold-fringed canopy of state over her head against the glare of the sun. All this at the height of the plague!

It is not hard to conclude from such an entrance that she knew her host well, and how best to impress him. Clement loved the company of beautiful women, and when the two finally met in the Consistory Hall word of her magnificent arrival would certainly have preceded her; Clement may well have observed her approach from a window of the papal palace. What we do know is that he straightaway arranged for a trial to be held in one of the great halls of the palace, with a throne raised on a dais at one end for the pope himself, and a semi-circle of cardinals seated around him at a lower level, robed in their full regalia. The prosecution was conducted by two ambassadors sent by King Louis of Hungary. Their evidence has not survived, but Queen Joanna's defence, which by all accounts she chose to conduct herself, was considered to have been a masterpiece of oratory, well supported—it was said inevitably—by her remarkable beauty. In any event Pope Clement seems to have had no hesitation in pronouncing her to be innocent of her husband's murder; and before long he had presented her with one of the greatest honours which the popes traditionally bestowed on only their most distinguished visitors, that masterpiece of the jeweller's art, the Golden Rose (see Chapter Seven).

Yet papal intervention in the dispute between Joanna and King Louis of Hungary came with a price. Not only did Joanna desperately need to be absolved of the crime of murder, she was also quite penniless. She had no means of returning to Naples to reclaim her kingdom even though she now had the pope's blessing. Clement duly obliged on both counts. Having declared her to be innocent of her former husband's murder, he proceeded to pay her the sum of 80,000 gold florins—in return for which he was enabled to take possession of the city which he had already done so much to make glorious.

And so, even as the plague continued to ravage the population of the city, and the cemeteries were running out of space for the dead, the sale of Avignon went through on 12 June of that year. The pope who had long rejoiced in living like a king at last had his kingdom.

This bare outline of events during the bleak summer of 1348 can make the deal with Queen Joanna sound cynical and exploitative on Clement's part. And it requires a framework of history to make it appear less so. The relationship between the rulers of Naples and the papacy had long been a very special one: in accordance with feudal laws they were actually vassals of the Holy See. Naples had accordingly been a staunch supporter of the popes in the continuous and acrimonious rivalry between the papacy and the Holy Roman Emperors over their respective powers within the Christian church. The current ruling family in Naples was French, like Clement himself; they were Angevins, from Anjou, and they were closely related to the Valois monarchs of France. They had seized the kingdom of Naples from the Aragonese earlier in the century, and had done so with the active support and blessing of the papacy. Before long the Neapolitan court became one of the most sophisticated in Europe. Writers, artists and philosophers flocked there. King Robert "the Wise" was a man described by Dante as "that fluent phenomenon", by

Petrarch as "a second Plato in intellect", and by Boccaccio as "the most learned king since Solomon". Both Petrarch and Boccaccio had delighted in Robert's friendship and boundless hospitality amid the splendours of his Castel Nuovo, with its summer houses, menageries, stabling and tireless entertainment. The Italian chronicler Villani described the monarch as "the wisest king that has been seen in Christendom for five hundred years".

But the Angevin rule in Naples had from the outset been bitterly disputed by another branch of the same family which (as a result of convoluted feudal match-making) had contrived to become rulers of Hungary. It had been an earlier Avignon pope, John XXII, who in his role as protector of the kingdom of Naples had attempted to heal this persistent feud between the rival Angevin factions by arranging a marriage between a scion from each family. Thus in September 1333, shortly before the aged Pope John died, two young royal pawns found themselves formerly engaged to one another. They were the seven-year-old Princess Joanna of Naples and the six-year-old Prince Andrew of Hungary. And twelve months afterwards the two children were duly married.

Nine years later, in 1343, just one year after Clement became pope, King Robert of Naples died. His two daughters and an only son had already died before him, and Robert's appointed heir was now his granddaughter Joanna. She was aged seventeen.

At this time of political instability throughout the whole of Italy Joanna's position as the youthful ruler of a disputed kingdom seemed desperately vulnerable. The Hungarian faction was poised to pounce on Naples at the slightest indication that their young prince might be receiving less than his due honours. It was at this moment that Pope Clement decided to assert his protective authority over the young queen in an attempt to forestall any eruption of violence. In August the following year, 1344, Joanna duly signed an oath of allegiance to the papacy, effectively making

Clement her guardian until she became of age. He appointed one of his cardinals as papal legate to administer the realm: but shortly afterwards, presumably on the advice of those who knew Joanna, he decided that she was mature enough to rule on her own, and withdrew the legate.

The next few years must often have made Clement doubt the wisdom of that decision. At the age of eighteen Joanna proceeded to rule her kingdom in what may best be described as a spirit of wilful and eccentric generosity. Like her celebrated grandfather she gloried in presiding over a court in which poets, artists, philosophers, doctors, mathematicians, astronomers and all manner of other learned people were always welcomed. She was the queen of all worldly pleasures, and she revelled in it all. Opinions varied about her moral probity. There were some who claimed she had no morals at all, and that she was the embodiment of every possible sensual vice. Others were enthralled by her beauty, and adored her for the warmth and joyfulness of her love of life. Her reputation spread rapidly across Europe, arousing the predictable gamut of responses. How many of the stories told about her were founded in truth is impossible to assess; for instance it was claimed that her principal lady-in-waiting, a certain Filipppa Catanese, was responsible for fostering the young queen's sensual appetites by supplying her with lovers, and in doing so for cultivating a growing aversion in her towards her boy of a husband.

True or not, this was certainly believed to be so by Andrew's family and hangers-on in Naples. They maintained that Joanna was increasingly excluding her husband from public events in favour, no doubt, of courtiers and (no doubt) lovers who pleased her a great deal more. Nor is this hard to imagine; not only was Andrew a mere boy, he was also cursed with a squint and was, in Petrarch's words, "from all eternity ugly and contemptible". None the less, ugly and cross-eyed though he might be, her reputed treatment of him was provoking mounting threats of reprisals by

Andrew's enraged family. Petrarch feared for her safety; she was a lamb, he wrote, "entrusted to the care of so many wolves."

Petrarch had every reason to fear for her. On the night of 18 September 1345 Joanna and her young husband Andrew were staying at the castle of Aversa, near Naples. Andrew was preparing for bed when he heard a voice call out to him with some urgency from outside the bedroom door. He dressed hurriedly and went out into the corridor where he was seized by a group of men, who gagged him to stifle his cries, and then strangled him with a silken cord. The crime was a hideous one; the prince's body was stripped, then dragged by his hair and genitals to an open window from where it was hanged from a balcony overlooking the park. Servants passing by at dawn rushed into the castle to report what they had seen.

The horrific murder of Andrew stunned even those many Neapolitans who had felt little affection for Joanna's young husband and even less for the lawless mob of Hungarian supporters who had descended on Naples in his wake. Joanna found herself widely held responsible for the crime, or at least for having instigated it. She herself insisted on her innocence, claiming to have been asleep in the bedroom at the time quite unaware of what was taking place in the corridor outside.

A further dubious complication occurred less than a week later when she gave birth to a son. Pope Clement, as Joanna's guardian, agreed to become the child's godfather, but there seems to have been rather less agreement on who might be the actual father. It was generally thought that the least likely candidate was her late husband. In any case the child rapidly disappeared from sight, and does not seem to have survived long.

By now Joanna was openly co-habiting in the royal palace with her first cousin, Robert of Taranto, though she very soon banished him from her bed in favour of his brother Louis of Taranto who, on the evidence of his grasping behaviour in the years to come, emerges as the most likely instigator of Andrew's murder. He was a man who wanted power, and was prepared to do anything to get it. He was one of the "wolves" whom Petrarch warned about.

Not surprisingly the long-standing acrimony between the two rival Angevin families, which Joanna's marriage was intended to heal, was by now combustible. Andrew's outraged elder brother, King Louis of Hungary, openly accused Joanna of adultery and murder, demanding that the "shameless queen" be deposed. And when she refused to leave he launched a military expedition to seize Naples. Fearing for her life, and accompanied by her newly-married husband Louis of Taranto, Joanna fled the city to seek the protection of the one man capable of restoring her reputation and her kingdom—Pope Clement.

These were the torrid circumstances in which Queen Joanna, penniless, homeless and accused of murder, rode through the streets of plague-ridden Avignon on a white stallion to be tried by a papal court, then to agree to sell her city to the man who had absolved her of that crime. It was one of the most poignant moments in the history of Avignon, and of the papacy in general.

The postscript to that moment in Avignon's history is no less dramatic than the events preceding it. In Joanna's absence King Louis of Hungary's invading troops committed so many atrocities in Naples that the population rose against them, and Louis himself left the city in some haste. But instead of a triumphant return to her kingdom Joanna now faced an even graver crisis as the saga of family treachery continued. Her husband Louis proceeded to seize power from her, and even threatened Joanna's life. Once again Pope Clement hurried to her aid. He despatched several galleys to Naples where his appointed legate succeeded in compelling Louis to hand power back to the queen. As her biographer E. G. Léonard has written, Clement continued to protect her "from her bad advisers, from her cousins, from the King of Hungary, from her husband, from almost the whole of Italy, and from public opinion."

Joanna's marital fortunes continued to be coloured by a mixture of eccentricity and disaster. After the treacherous Louis died she married the King of Majorca who was eleven years her junior and half-mad from having spent thirteen years of his young life imprisoned in an iron cage. Widowed for the third time in 1375, the following year she contracted a marriage by proxy to a German baron and military adventurer by the name of Otto of Brunswick, about whom little was subsequently heard. Having no surviving children Joanna now decided to appoint the brother of the king of France—yet another Louis—as her heir to the throne of Naples, thereby snubbing the man who considered himself to be her natural heir, Charles of Durazzo, cousin of her second former husband Louis of Taranto. True to family tradition Charles promptly seized power, had himself crowned King of Naples, and incarcerated Joanna in the remote mountain castle of Muro where in the following year his hired thugs broke into her room, bound her to the bedstead, and in a macabre replication of her first husband's murder, strangled her.

The castle of Muro Lucano still stands—a gaunt witness to the heroic tragedy of a woman whose way of life would have been brilliantly suited to eighteenth-century Paris or Venice, but whose way of death was all too typical of the brutish times in which she lived.

Pope Clement, who loved and admired Joanna, did more to help her than any man, not least because it was due to her that the papacy became not merely the tenant of Avignon, but its owner. But by the time of Joanna's death her papal guardian had himself been dead thirty years, and three further popes had come and gone. Ironically the city she had once sold to Clement was no longer the papal city: by then the popes were back in Rome. But that is for the final chapters of this book.

§

Eleven days after Clement presented Queen Joanna with the emblem of the Golden Rose another beautiful woman in Avignon died. The Black Death, which both the pope and Joanna survived, claimed the life of the lady Petrarch had adored from afar for twenty-one years. She was the legendary Laura.

Petrarch was in Italy at the time, in the city of Parma, where the plague was raging just as severely as it was in Avignon. As yet unaware of Laura's death, it was here in Parma that he heard of the remarkable survival of his younger brother Gherardo, the one who had climbed Mont Ventoux with him twelve years earlier. Gherardo had become a member of a religious community in Provence by the time the plague struck. After several months, so Petrarch learned, only he (and his dog) had survived out of a total of thirty-five inmates, all of whom he had helped to nurse, and ultimately to bury. It seemed that by some miracle Gherardo himself had been spared, and Petrarch wrote to him in astonishment and gratitude: "My brother, my beloved brother, what shall I say? On all sides is sorrow; everywhere is fear... Will posterity, if there is one, ever believe that without anyone having seen, either coming down from the sky or up out of the earth, a devouring fire, without war, without any visible cause of destruction, the world was almost completely depopulated?... Where are now our pleasant friends? Where are the loved faces? Where are their cheering words? Where their sweet and gentle conversation? We used to be surrounded by a crowd of intimates, but now we are almost alone."

One of the "intimates" who had perished in the plague was his friend and first patron, Cardinal Colonna. Then on 9 May Petrarch received a letter from one of those friends who had survived—Ludovicus (whom he called Socrates)—informing him of a death that cut him to the quick: that of his beloved Laura. She had in fact died more than a month earlier, on 6 April. By a piece of mystical coincidence, which Petrarch made much of later, her death had taken place at the same hour and on the very same day as when he had first met her twenty-one years before. "She died gently," he wrote, "without a struggle, not like a torch that has been put out, but like a light with nothing more to feed on."

And so the shadowy legend of Laura came to an end—Avignon's most famous lady about whom we know almost nothing. She is reputed to have been buried in one of the chapels of the Franciscan church attached to the Convent of the Cordeliers which was then in the process of reconstruction at the expense of Pope Clement. Whether her tomb was ever really there—whoever she was—will never be known for certain, though a notice today by the side of the gaunt bell-tower (virtually all that survives of the convent church) confidently claims as much. It was certainly widely believed to be true and continued as such; nearly two hundred years later King Francis I, patron of Leonardo da Vinci in his old age, came here to meditate and to savour the legend of Petrarch's undying passion.

Three years after her death, in 1351, Petrarch was drawn back to his retreat in the Vaucluse to be closer to his memories of her. "I never knew another valley," he wrote, "that preserved so many private places where one could sigh... I was seized by a longing to see again my hills and caves and groves carpeted with green moss and the ever-resonant rocks by the fountain of the Sorgues. Where I came as a boy, then as a youth, and again as a grown man, I have now returned when near to old age—though I have sworn never to come here again."

Here he recorded his memorial to Laura on the fly-leaf of his beloved copy of Virgil (now in the Ambrosiana Library, Milan). "The west wind comes, bringing back fair weather, bringing the grass and flowers... The meadows laugh, the sky is calm again. Air, water, earth are filled with love; each living being turns to love again. Alas, for me there are only sighs, the heavy sighs that she drags out of my heart, she who has carried its keys away to heaven. And the songs of little birds, and the flowers of the river banks, and the sweet gait of chaste and fair ladies, all these are but a desert to me."

The "desert", however, did manage to contain a well-organized household which included a devoted common-law wife and their two children. But then Petrarch's disembodied love for Laura never seems to have impinged upon the daily business of living, or interrupted his travels across Europe in search of fame and patronage. He carried his secret love like a secret miniature or a locket of hair wherever he went; and none of the lofty prelates and princes he met, and charmed, and impressed with his learning and his wit, would ever know it was there.

There was another considerably less romantic reason for Petrarch's decision to return to Avignon in that year. Mystery surrounds the precise circumstances, but it seems that Clement tried to tempt the great man back into the fold with a hint—or was it a promise?—of some lucrative appointment which would keep him in Avignon. Petrarch, always short of funds and forever hungry for fame, may have imagined that the offer would be nothing less than a cardinal's hat (his disdain of opulence would never have inhibited him from wearing scarlet). In the event the offer was rather more humdrum, the post of Apostolic Secretary, which would have been financially lucrative but heavily demanding of Petrarch's time. He managed to wriggle out of it, only to be offered a bishopric which would have been even more demanding; there would be no time for poetry, and no time for those restless journeys from one patron to another. Again he managed to refuse.

In 1353, again disillusioned, Petrarch left Vaucluse and Avignon, this time for good. His destination was Milan. And yet, physically though he may have abandoned Avignon, in his thoughts he seems to have remained closer to the place than when he actually lived there or in nearby Vaucluse. In the comfort of his fresh surroundings, basking in the hospitality of his new patron who was the powerful ruler of the city, Petrarch now devoted much of his energy to turning his love for the dead Laura into poetry. The result was the long sonnet sequence known as the *Canzoniere*, the literary destination for which Laura had always been best suited in Petrarch's mind. Death having removed her from reality, it was as if he was finally allowed to take possession of her soul.

There is one further twist to the story of Petrarch's choice of Milan as his new place of residence. Its rulers were the long-time enemies of Avignon, and one suspects there may have been a degree of malice on the poet's part in choosing to live there. His host, Giovanni Visconti, was the city's archbishop as well as its despotic ruler. He had been high on the list of Pope Clement's personal enemies, having exercised his territorial ambitions by annexing a large chunk of papal territory in northern Italy including the city of Bologna, thereby inviting an angry threat of excommunication from Clement—which Visconti had contemptuously brushed aside. In fact, in the lordliness of their behaviour, their persuasive charm and flamboyant enjoyment of life's pleasures the two men were remarkably similar—probably too alike to find space for one another in the same world. They were a pair of titans locked in bitter conflict. Inevitably, in the last years of his life Clement found himself expending all too much resourcefulness, as well as far too much of the papal treasury, on doing battle with the lord of Milan over those lost papal territories in Italy.

Though Clement died the year before Petrarch finally left Vaucluse and made his move to Milan, this is the moment to turn back the clock and look at some of those campaigns, both in Italy and in France, as well as further east in Asia Minor, into which Avignon was dragged willy-nilly during his papacy.

The Battle of Crécy, 1346, a cataclysmic defeat for the French at the hands of the English in the early stages of the Hundred Years War, in which the Avignon popes repeatedly tried to negotiate a peace treaty, mostly in vain.

9

The World Stage

With a newly-acquired city and a newly-built palace Pope Clement could well feel that the role he had been elected to play was becoming fulfilled. It was the role of a man who believed himself, without a shadow of doubt, to be sovereign and unchallengeable as the physical representative of God on this earth. He was the crowned king of Christendom. Avignon was the undisputed hub of his Christian world.

Such unwavering self-assurance left little room for humility; but then humility was never a prevailing quality in Clement's make-up. The absence of it made him especially sensitive to any threats to that supreme authority which he was so proud to claim, and during his pontificate there were a great many such threats. His more self-effacing predecessor, Benedict, had inclined towards conciliation in dealing with opponents; by contrast Clement preferred to confront them head-on. At the same time he was by nature a diplomat, not a warrior, and where possible he chose to fight his wars with his wits rather than on the battlefield. Many of his notable successes on the world stage came from employing those sharp mental weapons. It was not for nothing that he had long been respected (and often feared) for possessing one of the finest brains in France, and that even as pope he continued to be among the most trusted advisers to the French king.

The most conspicuous of these diplomatic successes was his triumph over the Holy Roman Emperor, Louis of Bavaria. Successive German emperors had pursued a belligerent policy against the papacy, maintaining that since they were the natural heirs of Charlemagne the temporal authority of the church lay with them rather than with the popes, who as bishops of Rome should only concern themselves with spiritual matters: in other words they should content themselves with saying mass and pronouncing on matters of theology, leaving worldly affairs to men of this world. Accordingly, over the preceding three centuries there had been a long-standing battle between emperors and popes over what powers each had a right to wield, and therefore who was the effective head of Latin Christendom.

Pope Clement harboured no doubts at all on this score: the pope was the head of Christendom, and that was that. Louis of Bavaria, who had previously led an army to Rome and had himself crowned emperor in St. Peter's (see Chapter Three), was in Clement's eyes an impostor and an arrogant threat to papal authority. The pope's celebrated sermons, delivered in Avignon's ancient cathedral, have survived, and they make stirring reading. In claiming powers for the emperor which rightly belonged to the pope Louis was guilty of "rending the seamless garment of Christ in two... placing two heads on one body," Clement thundered. He had no hesitation whatever in describing the emperor as "a rabid dog, a devouring wolf, a fetid he-goat, and a cunning serpent". These were hardly the words of a diplomat, but none the less Clement sensed he was on the winning side. Louis' star was fading; in Italy his power and influence were already severely diminished, while north of the Alps squabbling German barons were undermining his power base. Clement in his persuasive way was adept at taking advantage of such divisions, playing one baron off against another and accruing personal support through a shrewd blend of bullying and bribery. The Germans were no match for the pope's tactical brain, and his final coup in 1346 was to engineer overwhelming support for the appointment of a rival to the emperor in the person of a young nobleman who so happened to have been recently received and royally entertained as a personal guest of Clement in Avignon's papal palace. The nobleman was Charles of Moravia, and he accordingly became appointed king of the Romans, thereby precipitating Louis' final downfall and in all probability hastening his death the following year.

It was a personal triumph for Clement, and it marked the end for ever of German imperial power extending south of the Alps. Nor was there ever again any question of a German emperor being able to call himself the head of Christendom. The pope might be temporarily "exiled" in Avignon, but Latin Christendom was still his empire, and it was now his alone.

On the darker side, within the papal territories in Italy threats to papal authority were growing ever more dangerous and more widespread. It was now forty years since the popes had abandoned Rome, and in that time the absence of papal government in the city had allowed a variety of adventurers to fill the vacuum. The most notable of these during Clement's pontificate was the son of a Roman innkeeper by the name of Nicola Di Lorenzo, which he soon shortened to Cola di Rienzo. As a young man Cola rose to fame on the wave of successes gained by the Roman popular party which was dedicated, somewhat fancifully, to the cause of restoring imperial Rome's greatness. It was as a representative of this new populist government that Cola was sent to Avignon as part of a delegation to plead for the pope's support for the party and to beg for the return of the papacy to Rome so that it would become a champion of that city's rebirth. While not acceding to Cola's request the pope was none the less impressed by the young man's zeal and duly appointed him notary of the Roman civic treasury— a somewhat hollow accolade since the treasury contained almost nothing. On his return to Rome fantasies of the city's glorious past began to go to Cola's head. He provoked a popular revolution in which he presented himself as the saviour of all Italy, only to become seen in a very short time as a self-serving demagogue. He soon found himself denounced as a criminal, a pagan and a heretic by the very pope who had previously honoured him. Forced to resign, Cola went into hiding before fleeing to Prague, where the archbishop proceeded to deliver him to Pope Clement.

The subsequent brief fame and downfall of Cola di Rienzo live on as much in the realm of legend as of history, and belong to the period immediately following that of Pope Clement. Absolved by the Inquisition of the charge of heresy, Cola enjoyed a triumphant return to Rome in 1354 with the blessing of Clement's successor, Innocent VI, only to be confronted within two months by a mob driven to fury by his arbitrary rule. Cola attempted to escape in disguise, but was recognized, seized and murdered. Five centuries later his buccaneering career found its apotheosis in the imagination of nineteenth-century Romantic writers forever hungry for vainglorious heroes. Cola became the subject of a melodramatic English novel of 1835 by E. G. Bulwer-Lytton, the book winning fame enough in its day to catch the eye of a poverty-stricken Richard Wagner who transformed the story into what became his first major professional success, an opera entitled simply *Rienzi*.

The Cola di Rienzo affair was a relatively minor storm compared to the tempests that continually battered Pope Clement in his dealings with Italy in general. In Avignon he could enjoy the pomp and grandeur of being the spiritual head of

Christendom to whom world leaders came to pay court and enjoy the celebrated papal hospitality; but the task of retaining control of papal lands abroad was quite a different matter. Even when the seat of the papacy had been Rome successive popes had still found it well-nigh impossible to keep a firm grip on the papal territories that were scattered throughout the peninsula, but now that seat lay outside Italy altogether the task was far harder. The belligerent Pope John thirty years earlier had felt compelled to spend more than sixty per cent of the entire papal revenues on mounting wars in Italy. John's successor, Benedict, managed to reduce that expenditure by scarcely engaging in military campaigns at all, as a result of which the territories in Italy slipped even further into anarchy, control falling increasingly into the hands of a variety of grasping local lords. For Clement it was a crippling inheritance, and not surprisingly he found himself even more heavily committed than John had been. Some indication of the scale of that commitment lies in the fact that, profligate though Clement's spending on the luxuries of the papal court may have been, the cost was still less than he was forced to spend on waging wars in Italy. In all, Clement's financial commitments were heavy in the extreme, and they bled the papal treasury consistently throughout his reign. To suggest that Clement lived above his income would be a grotesque understatement. But then he preferred to "live like a king." Matters of finance were for lesser mortals.

The papal territories in Italy had been acquired over the centuries, originally as a bulwark against barbarian invasions from both north and south, but more recently through the customary feudal practices of tactical marriages and family inheritance. The territories—seven of them—were widely spread, effectively filling the area of Italy between the former Holy Roman Empire in the north and the kingdom of Naples in the south. They consisted of the Romagna in the north, the city and county of Bologna, the district of Ancona on the east coast, the Duchy of Spoleto in central Italy, the regions around Rome known as the Campagna and Maritima, and the town

and territory of Benevento further south. Responsibility for administering these areas now rested with French officials who had been appointed by the popes—misguidedly so. Not speaking the language and with no local experience, these officials had virtually without exception proved grossly incompetent or grossly corrupt, and frequently both. Papal control in these areas had become little more than nominal.

Unless all papal lands except the Comtat in Provence were to be lost for ever Pope Clement had no choice but to take up arms—not a course of action for which he had any natural talent.

The most troublesome of these Italian states was the most northerly: Romagna, today Emilia-Romagna, and in particular the province and city of Bologna which lay within the territory of Romagna. Papal authority here had already withered away by the time Clement decided to take action. His chief protagonist was that arch-enemy of the Avignon papacy, Giovanni Visconti, the ruler of Milan as well as its archbishop, whose territorial ambitions included seizing as much papal territory as possible in order to carve out a powerful state for himself in northern and central Italy.

The Visconti had been the ruling family in Milan for more than two centuries, having transformed the title of "viscount of

Milan" into their own surname. As a family they had formed the habit of living colourful and dangerous lives. Giovanni Visconti had become the sole lord of Milan in 1349 after his brother Lucchino was murdered by his wife Isabella. Giovanni himself (as touched on in the previous chapter) was a man who succeeded in combining unscrupulous ambition with great charisma and personal charm: hence perhaps the mutual respect and affection which he and Petrarch came to feel for one another when the latter became his guest in Milan. Politically Visconti was in that rare position of being a match for Clement: as a churchman on the other hand he made the pope appear a veritable saint. Being the city's archbishop meant little more to him than providing another seat of power. He is said to have celebrated mass only once in his life, and on that occasion to have managed to drop the host. He was heard to declare proudly that in any case the host was only a piece of unleavened bread, and as for the wine it was merely the fermented juice of the grape. "I prefer to eat tasty dishes and drink good wine," he added. Surrounded by a court of at least six hundred people, Giovanni Visconti, like Clement, chose to live like a prince.

But it was Visconti's political ambitions rather than his overblown lifestyle or lack of religious principles that brought him into direct conflict with Pope Clement. Visconti had his eye on as number of strategic cities. One of these was the great port of Genoa which would enable him to have access to the sea on both side of the Italian peninsula. And if he was to extend his domain southwards from Lombardy towards Tuscany then he would need a headquarters from which to launch himself into central Italy; and the ideal stepping-stone was the city of Bologna, still officially papal territory even though papal authority had long since crumbled away.

There followed a series of moves and countermoves. In October 1350 Giovanni contrived to annex the city of Bologna. By this time he had already annexed Genoa, and so the burgeoning Milanese state was beginning to stare hungrily at Tuscany and the whole of central Italy, the papal states in particular. Now Giovanni's nephew (and successor) Galeazzo chose to march into Bologna with an army. This was the final provocation, and it was at this point that Pope Clement delivered Giovanni his threat of excommunication, which the Milanese ruler contemptuously ignored. History rarely offers a clear explanation for a rebuttal of this kind. Did the prospect of being anathematized, placed outside the embrace of God, condemned to perpetual damnation, make no impact on a man even though he was a high-ranking servant of the church? Was Visconti, with his scorn for the sacred rituals of the church, at heart a non-believer for whom a threat of this magnitude therefore meant nothing at all? Or was he simply calling the pope's bluff, provoking Clement to take military action against him, suspecting (rightly) that he would be likely to win?

If it was provocation then it was shrewd of Visconti. Clement duly raised an army against him, but it was one that soon proved to be insufficient in numbers, ill-equipped, and for long periods of time unpaid. The pope simply had no money; he was living perilously on loans. The expedition became a disaster, and Clement felt compelled to negotiate with Visconti. In September 1351 discussions took place in Avignon, Giovanni no doubt happy to concede to the pope's summons knowing that he had the whip hand. Concessions were made on his part, but these turned out to be hollow; Visconti magnanimously agreed to restore Bologna into papal hands, but at the same time he obtained from Clement the right to keep control of the city for a further twelve years. In other words papal dominion over Bologna would remain little more than a fiction.

It was now that a piece of unexpected good fortune came Clement's way—or perhaps it was a case of smart opportunism on the pope's part. A churchman who was in every way as ruthless and as cunning as Giovanni Visconti suddenly came to Clement's aid, at least potentially so. He was a Spaniard by the name of Gil Alvarez Carrillo de Albornoz. Related to the royal family of Castile, Albornoz was a lawyer and churchman who had become Archbishop of Toledo and chancellor of the kingdom of Castile while still in his twenties. But besides these prestigious appointments he had another profession: he was a brilliant soldier. In the course of the 1340s he had won a series of decisive battles against the Saracens in southern Spain. His reputation as the outstanding general of his day reached the ears of the papal court in Avignon at just the time when events in Italy were rendering Pope Clement desperately in need of a skilled military brain. It was at this fortuitous moment that Albornoz fell foul of the then new ruler of Castile, King Pedro II, known for good reason as "the Cruel". Whether by papal invitation or by the Spaniard's own choice remains unclear, but the immediate outcome of the quarrel was that in 1350 Albornoz took refuge in Avignon.

Regardless of whether Clement was personally responsible, the arrival in the papal city of the most renowned soldier of his day was nothing less than a blessing for a beleaguered pope. And perhaps in order to make quite sure that Albornoz remained in the papal service Clement promptly made him a cardinal.

The subsequent career of this military archbishop and cardinal spans the pontificate of Clement's successors as pope. For the moment it is sufficient to say that the papacy's overall debt to Albornoz was to become immense. Not only did he succeed in driving the Visconti family out of Bologna, but in the course of the following ten years he also succeeded in subduing the feudal despots and warlords who for so long had been controlling the different papal states in Italy.

It was as a direct result of these achievements that the seventh and last of the Avignon popes was eventually able to feel confident enough to return to Rome. But these events, and the military exploits of the remarkable Cardinal Albornoz, belong to later chapters of this book.

§

Like all the Avignon popes Clement VI inherited a far greater threat to the security of Christendom than the operations of a few Italian warlords. For five hundred years European rulers, as well as church leaders, had been obsessed with the territorial ambitions of Islam. And not unreasonably so; after two-and-a-half centuries the crusading movement had run its course, and in the end had achieved nothing. There was no longer a Crusader Kingdom in the Levant, and Jerusalem itself lay in Muslim hands. The only military achievements against Islam of any consequence were in Spain where the Reconquest now accounted for the greater part of the Iberian Peninsula, but elsewhere there had been little for a Christian to celebrate. The Ottoman Turks were now perceived as the greatest menace. A vast Turkish sultanate had come to control most of the Eastern Mediterranean, embracing Egypt, Syria, all the Bible lands including Jerusalem, and most of Asia Minor where its tentacles had now reached as far as the Bosphorus, facing Constantinople and the continent of Europe just across the narrow waters. Pockets of Christian authority still survived, among them Armenia, and there were a few island strongholds, principally Cyprus which had been held by the French Lusignan dynasty since the Third Crusade, and Rhodes which was occupied by the Knights of St. John of Jerusalem, the Knights Hospitallers, since their retreat from the Holy Land in 1306. The only supremacy enjoyed by the Christian powers was at sea, and even here Turkish pirate vessels were in the habit of making devastating raids.

This was the political map which Clement inherited. Born in the year Acre fell—the last Christian outpost in the Bible lands— he had lived with the failure of the crusading enterprise all his life. He was far too realistic a man to envisage mounting yet another military excursion to the Levant; there was neither the will, nor the money nor the manpower. Besides, with two major powers, England and France, locked in an interminable conflict there was no possibility of coordinating any such expedition. An air of futility had come to permeate the whole crusading dream.

At the same time a messianic passion to do something persisted in the minds of European rulers. Clement was no cynic; he was not a man who could simply shrug off the deep longing which every Christian leader continued to feel to restore Christ's homeland to Christendom. He also genuinely feared the consequences of doing nothing at all to combat Islam. He delivered one of his celebrated sermons on the subject, voicing the dread that the Saracens would soon reach as far as Naples if no attempt was made to stop them. And in 1344 he wrote to the Knights Hospitallers in Rhodes that "the ferocious and abominable Turks aimed to shed Christian blood" with the purpose of extinguishing "the very name of Christianity". For Clement it was a question of what action might be feasible, however small it might be. Yet another crusading disaster would also be a disaster for the Avignon papacy.

In the spring of the same year, 1344, Clement pulled off another of his diplomatic triumphs. He won an agreement between the rulers of the Venetian Republic, the king of Cyprus and the Grand Master of the Knights of Rhodes to create a naval league whose purpose would be to defend Christian outposts in the Middle East against the Turks. This was a far less ambitious undertaking than any full-scale crusade, but it was realistic, like the man who conceived it. The first objective of the league was to recapture the port of Smyrna (Izmir in modern Turkey) on the Aegean coast of what was then the emirate of Anatolia, and which had become the principal Turkish base for launching piratical raids throughout the Eastern Mediterranean. Clement undertook to supply four galleys at the papacy's cost, to be launched presumably from Marseille. Four more galleys were offered by the king of

Cyprus, six by the Knights Hospitallers on the island of Rhodes, and a further six by the Republic of Venice and her numerous Greek colonies. With remarkable speed the fleet of twenty galleys was assembled and headed for the Turkish coast. With the advantage of surprise, on 28 October that same year the port of Smyrna was successfully captured.

In the context of the crusading movement as a whole this was a small victory, yet within Christendom it did much for the morale and prestige of the Avignon papacy and for Pope Clement in particular. He had shown himself to be a true leader. As with his strategy for outmanoeuvring the German emperor, the formation of the naval league demonstrated that one of his great strengths lay in his powers of persuasion. It was no accident that Clement had the ear of virtually every ruler in Europe, even those, like Giovanni Visconti in Milan, who were in a strong enough position to get the better of him.

Flushed with the success of the Smyrna operation, Clement felt able to write of his determination to pursue "the defence and extension of the Faith in Anatolia". In fact this was not to be; and the aftermath of the Smyrna triumph was a good deal less than glorious. The Turks retaliated by mounting a raid in which they managed to kill three of the league's leaders. The league's impetus rapidly faltered. Smyrna itself hung on as a Christian outpost (until Tamerlaine seized it half a century later), but it was never anything but isolated, vulnerable and poor. Within four years the league's galleys were no longer operating, and in 1351 the league came to an end altogether.

With the Smyrna expedition the torch of the crusading movement had flickered for almost the last time. Small military triumphs would follow in the decades to come, all of them ultimately of no significance. It seems appropriate that the most forceful of the seven Avignon popes should at least have had a hand in the last positive achievement of the crusading movement.

In the thirty years to follow all three of Clement's successors would make pious noises about mounting yet another military expedition, but those noises soon blew away on the winds. And the reason—or the excuse—was always the same: what we have come to know as the Hundred Years War.

§

It may have been a myth, and had it been put to the test very possibly it would have proved to be one. Even so, it was a conviction which Pope Clement and his successors all firmly held, namely that if only the long-dragged-out war between France and England could be peacefully terminated then the crusading dream might once again come alive.

The first serious clashes between the two nations had taken place a decade before Clement became pope. King Charles IV of France had died without an heir. It was the end of the Capetian dynasty. The English king Edward III, who already owned Aquitaine, now demanded the French throne on the grounds that his mother was the dead king's sister and the daughter of King Philip the Fair; therefore he was in direct line of descent with a more legitimate claim than that of his French rival, Philip of Valois, who was merely the grandson of an earlier monarch, and furthermore only through a younger branch of the family. On such quibbling contentions was the Hundred Years War launched. A French assembly called to settle the issue not unnaturally chose one of their own, who duly became Philip VI. The new French king proceeded somewhat unwisely to confiscate part of English-owned Aquitaine, provoking an irate King Edward to cross the Channel with an army. The year 1337 has thus become the "official" date of the beginning of the Hundred Years War.

Over the next few years hostilities sputtered on fitfully, achieving little and draining both nations of material and financial resources. By the time Clement became pope in 1342 the war had already lasted for five years inconclusively, with neither side capable of breaking the deadlock. Up until that moment Clement himself had been a powerless witness. As a cardinal archbishop there had been little he could do but watch in mounting frustration. Suddenly, as pope, his exasperation found its voice. Unlike his predecessor Benedict, who was always more concerned to crush heretics than resolve wars, Clement was a political animal who saw the role of pope as that of a peacemaker—one who might also, as a result of his efforts, be able to harness those wasted military resources and turn them against the Infidel. There lay the dream, or the myth.

It is easy to become dazzled by the hedonism and glamour of Clement's years as pope, and even the most academic of commentators on his papacy have tended to emphasize the more colourful aspects of his reign. In fact one thread which runs unbroken through the entire ten years of his papacy is the least glamorous aspect of it, namely his consistent search for peace between England and France. Avignon lay beyond the boundaries of both countries, and Clement saw the papal city not only as a seat of power, but as a seat of justice, as the ideal place where mediation could take place. The papal palace was where world leaders could meet and to talk, and where Clement, the most regal of popes, could employ his unique authority to offer them the peace of God.

Indeed, on the face of it Clement appeared to be the ideal figure to negotiate a lasting peace between England and France. He knew personally and liked both rulers, respectively Philip VI of France and Edward III of England. In his younger days Clement had been a courtier in the service of the French king, and before the outbreak of hostilities had visited England as a royal ambassador in 1328, and three years later, by now Archbishop of Rouen, had met and become friendly with the English monarch. A measure of his commitment to the cause of peace is the fact that a mere two weeks after being crowned pope he appointed two cardinals as papal nuncios with powers to negotiate a truce between the two nations. A year later a temporary truce was actually achieved; then in October the following year, when the conflict had once again escalated, Clement summoned representatives of both England and France to a conference in Avignon in a further bid to bring an end to hostilities.

With hindsight it seems inevitable that the talks should have broken down. Clement was far from being an impartial judge; he was a Frenchman, fundamentally loyal to his country and to his king, at whose court in Paris he had first shone and risen to eminence. Whatever pretence at detachment he may have displayed it would have been abundantly clear to the English contingent in those Avignon talks that their host regarded King Edward's claim to the throne of France as quite untenable, and the very presence of English soldiers on French soil as an act of aggression. And if further proof of the pope's bias were needed, it would have become known to the English that over the five years between 1345 and 1350 Clement repeatedly lent (i.e. gave) large sums of money to King Philip, each loan resulting in a renewed burst of military activity by the French. It would also have been known, furthermore, that the pope had allowed the French king the "tenths" of all ecclesiastical income for two years, a privilege only allowed once before, and that was by Pope John, the purpose on that occasion being to help finance a crusade. Moreover it was a privilege later denied to the king of England. Not surprisingly Clement's repeated attempts to broker peace were doomed.

Clement's loyal support for King Philip also proved of little avail. On 26 August 1346 the French army suffered a cataclysmic defeat at Crécy, north of Paris, at the hands of King Edward and his son Edward the Black Prince. The English longbowmen were largely responsible for the deaths of some fifteen hundred mounted French knights and squires, Among the dead were the

French king's brother, Charles of Alençon, as well as two of his chief allies, the king of Bohemia and the count of Flanders. King Philip himself was wounded.

Four years later, in 1350, Philip too was dead, and was succeeded by his son John, who became King John II, known as "the Good". Clement's own continuing loyalty to the French crown was rewarded by a royal visit to Avignon within a few months of the new king's coronation. This proved to be an occasion for one of Clement's widely-famed celebrations on a grand scale. For the city of Avignon it was a timely moment for such an event. Barely two years had passed since the Black Death had run its course. Now, as if to bury that disaster along with the thousands of dead which it had claimed, the city once again became a scene of pageantry, feasting and self-indulgence. And at the heart of the celebrations the young French king processed from the papal palace to the cathedral where in the company of the pope he ceremonially stood as godfather to Clement's infant niece. It was like the meeting of two monarchs.

Clement himself died shortly before Christmas 1352. He was sixty-one. The Florentine chronicler Matteo Villani, brother of the more distinguished Giovanni Villani, claimed (without quoting his authority) that the pope had been the victim of a venereal disease brought about by his immoral life. Clement himself had made no secret of his moral laxity; in a statement of confession a year before his death, echoed in a subsequent sermon, he admitted that he had lived as a sinner among sinners. There can be little doubt that those who attached themselves to the papal court seeking an example of moral rectitude in their pontiff must have had to turn many a blind eye, even if they fulminated less hotly then Petrarch ("Prostitutes swarm on the papal beds"). But whatever may have been Clement's excesses history has generally treated him more appreciatively than any of the other Avignon popes, giving precedence to his magnanimity and to the sheer grandeur of his personality over his moral peccadilloes. His most recent biographer, Diana Wood, not one given to eulogies, has written of Clement's legacy that he built up Avignon "as an intellectual and cultural hub of the Christian world".

Certainly the papal city would never see his like again; and until the supremacy of the Renaissance popes in sixteenth-century Rome no head of the Christian church would again appear so much larger than life. To many who had been part of his papal court in Avignon it must have seemed that his death was like the passing of an emperor.

Grandiose military showmanship by the kings of France: the twin-tower entrance to the Tour St.-André in Villeneuve, outstaring the papal city from across the Rhône.

10

Battles and Battlements

Pope Clement left Avignon looking splendid, but close to bankruptcy. The glories of his new palace concealed a room that was almost empty: the treasury. It had been Clement's hand which had always controlled the papal purse, and his hand which had emptied it. For ten years his rule had been that of an extravagantly generous autocrat. If he had deigned to consult his cardinals at all on matters of church and state it was generally only to seek assurance that he had been right all along. Hence it was no surprise that the cardinals who made up the Sacred College chose to follow a well-established tradition in Avignon, which was to elect a new pope who was as unlike his predecessor as possible—and in this instance someone who was also unlikely to ignore them for much of the time, thereby belittling their cherished role as princes of the church. The cardinals did not want another autocrat who would make them feel like mere factotums.

Their chosen candidate was far from being one of their own: he was the head of the Carthusian Order, a body of hermit-like monks who for the past two-and-a-half centuries had been pursuing their ascetic vocation in the silence of the high Alps north of Grenoble, at the monastery of La Grande Chartreuse, as far from the wickedness of the world as it was possible to get. But by a twist of irony the cardinals were so successful in having elected Clement's total opposite that their chosen man declined to accept the papacy out of sheer humility.

So the cardinals were compelled to try again. This time they played safe and elected a fellow-cardinal. He was yet another southern Frenchman, Etienne Aubert, an elderly churchman who had been a professor of law at Toulouse, then on taking orders had held several bishoprics in France, and in the year of Clement's death had been appointed Cardinal-Bishop of Ostia, in the papal states outside Rome. The fifth Avignon pope took the title Innocent VI.

It is not recorded how many of the cardinals may soon have regretted their choice of successor to Clement. Keen though they may have been to be given a greater say in the affairs of the church, they would have been equally anxious to retain the luxurious lifestyle they had grown accustomed to enjoy under the previous regime. But Innocent was a sober and prudent man, and his first instinct was to balance the books. Expenditure had spiralled out of control in Clement's day; living like a king had meant behaving as if money descended directly from heaven by royal right. Innocent changed all that. He carried out draconian reforms within the papal court, dismissing numerous flunkies and parasites who had installed themselves there, and insisting that priests return to the parishes on whose revenues they were cynically living. He also drastically reduced the staff of the papal palace, curtailing most of the luxuries which had come to be taken for granted by the papal entourage. And he put an end to the continual feasting and carousing for which Avignon had become notorious throughout Europe.

Like many of the Avignon cardinals Innocent had already built a handsome residence on the far side of the Rhône, in Villeneuve, directly across the river and linked to Avignon by the twenty-two arches of the Pont St.-Bénézet. By this time there were at least fifteen such *livrées*, erected on land relinquished to the papal authorities from the former owners at an undisclosed cost. Although on French rather than papal territory Villeneuve offered the benefit of available space for building, which had become increasingly hard to find in overcrowded and less than hygienic Avignon.

One of Innocent's most surprising decisions on being elected pope was to offer his *livrée* to the Carthusians, then proceeding to convert and expand it into a monastery largely at his own expense. Innocent had no apparent connections with the Carthusians, and the most likely explanation for this act of generosity is the wave of gratitude he may have felt towards the head of the Carthusian order for having declined the papacy, but for which Innocent himself would still have been Cardinal-Bishop of Ostia in hostile Italy, an appointment no one accustomed to the relative tranquillity of Avignon would have welcomed. It also seems probable that a man who was zealously curbing the excesses of the papal court would have warmed to the Spartan ethic of the Carthusians, who were the one religious body in Christendom which had managed to maintain its iron disciplines without ever lapsing into softer ways and needing to be reformed.

The conversion of Innocent's *livrée* into a charterhouse took a little more than three years to complete. The chapel became the monastery's church, consecrated in 1358. The banqueting hall was transformed into the monks' refectory. Extra sleeping accommodation was added, together with a new cloister, as well as practical facilities such as a laundry, a bakery and—naturally—a cemetery. Finally, when Innocent decided he wished to be buried here (which in 1362 he was), an extra chapel was built to house his tomb.

And so the former cardinal's mansion became known as the Chartreuse Pontificale du Val-de-Bénédiction. The place was expanded greatly after Innocent's day, initially by one of the pope's nephews and subsequently by a sequence of cardinals and noble families who continued to donate handsome sums of money over the following centuries, until by the seventeenth century the monastery had become the wealthiest charterhouse in France—

an ironic departure from the ascetic life in the snowbound Alps which had been chosen by the founder of the Carthusian order, St. Bruno, in the eleventh century.

Today the charterhouse (now a cultural centre) remains one of the most handsome spectacles of Villeneuve. By contrast, from the rear of the former monastery rises another spectacle, also erected in Pope Innocent's time. Half a century earlier King Philip the Fair, the monarch who effectively appointed the first Avignon pope, had constructed a castle bristling with turrets overlooking Avignon from across the river (the Tour Philippe-le-Bel being the one tower to survive). Now his successors, first John "the Good" then Charles "the Wise", undertook to construct a fort even more massive on the hill behind the charterhouse overlooking the Rhône and Avignon on the far side. Known as the Fort St.-André, it swallowed up a twelfth-century Benedictine monastery on the same hill, and with its colossal walls and gigantic twin towers striding the entrance it remains to this day one of the most awesome medieval fortifications in the whole of France. Like Philip the Fair's castle it was built to show royal muscle. It was an impregnable frontier post, and it was intended to outstare the papal city from the borders of French territory. Even though relations between the papacy and the French monarchy were now close and cordial, a certain bellicose tradition persisted when it came to France safeguarding its borders. For the most part the Fort St.-André was a piece of grandiose military showmanship.

The skyline of Avignon itself also changed dramatically in the decade of Innocent's papacy. Increasingly it was becoming the city of soaring Gothic belfries—which it has remained to this day. St.-Didier, the best-preserved of the medieval Avignon churches, with its pitted and craggy bell-tower, was rebuilt at this time at the expense of a French cardinal and decorated with Florentine frescoes in one of the chapels. Close by, the church of Nôtre-Dame-la-Principale, with its slender spire matching those above

the entrance to the papal palace, was also enlarged during this period. But the most flamboyant of the city's belfries is the one that rises above what is today the town hall, the Hôtel de Ville, on Avignon's main square. Known as the Tour du Jacquemart and spiky with gargoyles, it is all that remains of the *livrée* built by another of the French cardinals. He was Pope Innocent's nephew who became Cardinal Aubert, and who—perhaps in gratitude to his uncle for having appointed him—had the papal coat of arms carved into the keystone of the tower.

§

Pope Innocent inherited not only an outrageously expensive papal court in Avignon but an even more expensive military campaign in Italy. In order to finance the latter he was reduced to disposing of quantities of jewellery and melting down many of the spectacular gold and silver ornaments which had accumulated during the glittering years of Clement's pontificate.

Innocent's determination to balance Avignon's books was matched by an equal determination to regain control of the papal territories in the Italian peninsula. This was always going to be an uphill task. All previous efforts to reassert papal authority in Italy had proved a costly failure. There had been neither the resources nor the will. But now Innocent was able to make an opportunist move which was soon to alter the course of papal history, eventually signalling the end of Avignon as the seat of the papacy.

For the chance to make this move Innocent owed much to his predecessor. Clement VI had ensured that the papacy retained the services—should they be needed—of the Spanish lawyer-turned-churchman-turned-soldier Gil Alvarez Carillo de Albornoz. Albornoz had latterly fallen foul of the new ruler of Castile and taken refuge in Avignon, whereupon Clement had shrewdly made him a cardinal. Now, in one of the first appointments he made as pope, Innocent appointed Albornoz papal legate and vicar-general for Italy, placing him in charge of all military operations in the peninsula, his special brief being to subdue the feudal warlords who had grabbed the papal territories.

The soldier-cardinal duly left Avignon in August 1353, in the first year of Innocent's pontificate, and his military operations began that December against the rebel states in central Italy. Albornoz immediately displayed his diplomatic skills by securing the support—surprisingly—of that sworn enemy of Avignon, Giovanni Visconti, the ruler of Milan. Perhaps two militant archbishops were able to find much in common, or else in this instance mutual advantage overcame traditional hostility. In addition Albornoz obtained further help from the rulers of Parma, Piacenza, Pisa, Florence, Siena and Perugia, so crucially boosting his hitherto inadequate military resources and even less adequate finances.

Over the course of the next three years, in spite of frequent setbacks, one Italian rebel city after another fell to Albornoz: Orvieto, Viterbo, Spoleto, Rimini, Ancona, and finally the region of Romagna. His military success was frequently against the odds, and often brought about by what may be described as high-class diplomatic bribery. Instead of punishing defeated warlords Albornoz made a practice of offering them favours too lucrative to be refused, thereby ensuring their craven allegiance to the papal cause and minimizing the risk of being knifed in the back the moment his armies moved elsewhere. Hence some of the most unprincipled tyrants in Italy found themselves saddled with the title "papal vicar", and even occupying lofty ranks in the papal army. One such fallen warlord was Giovanni di Vico whose career in treachery had begun with the murder of his brother, and who then seized the cities of Orvieto and Viterbo from the papal authorities—this being in 1353, shortly before Albornoz' arrival in Italy. The following year Albornoz besieged Viterbo, finally compelling di Vico to surrender and beg for peace. The papal general proceeded to return all the warlord's goods and rights to him on the condition that he swear an oath of allegiance to the Holy See and undertake not to enter Viterbo for ten years. And as an assurance that these conditions would be kept, Albornoz took di Vico's son as a hostage. As a peace-making strategy it generally seemed to work.

The hardest nut to crack was the city of Bologna, which for some time had been unlawfully under the control of the lords of Milan. Giovanni Visconti, with whom Albornoz had formed an unlikely alliance in 1354, had died that same year. Now the chief reins of power in Milan were held by one of Giovanni's nephews, Bernabo Visconti. And Bernabo had no intention of giving up Bologna, as the city was a crucial platform for his expansionist ambitions. Albornoz was equally intractable, and the papal armies besieged the city. Bernabo continued to hope that negotiations might bring about a favourable compromise, but Albornoz adamantly refused to negotiate.

Bernabo then resorted to a different tactic. He despatched emissaries to Avignon armed with malicious gossip concerning the papal general's unreasonable intransigence and suspect motives. Pope Innocent, ever politically naïve, was taken in, almost certainly aided by a handsome bribe; and in March 1357 the pope sacked Albornoz, insisting on his return to Avignon. Then, in a display of even more crass political naïveté, Innocent appointed in the general's place a man with no military or organizational experience whatsoever. He was a cardinal by the name of Androin de la Roche, a simple and disingenuous figure whose only knowledge of the rough world was from the perspective of being abbot of the great Burgundian monastery of Cluny, and even this high office was scarcely more than nominal since he lived mostly in Avignon enjoying the good life. Predictably within a year the appointment to Italy proved a comprehensive disaster both militarily and in every other respect. After dithering and changing his mind several times the pope eventually admitted his mistake and reappointed Albornoz, sending him back to Italy to sort out the chaos which the inept abbot had left behind.

The struggle for the control of Bologna continued for two further years. Finally in March 1360 Albornoz' nephew Blasco Fernandez led a detachment of papal troops into the city, and the Visconti domination was over. There were many skirmishes to come in the following years, most of them inconclusive; yet the overall achievements of Albornoz in his years in Italy meant that the authority of the Holy See in the papal states was never again seriously threatened. The local warlords were either crushed or bought off. As a result the long dark tunnel of papal exile now had a light at the end of it—a dim light as yet, but at least the two Avignon popes who were to follow Innocent could consider a return to Rome as something more than an all-but-forgotten dream.

§

There were other wars during Innocent's ten-year reign which involved Avignon more directly, and far more painfully, than the struggles for papal control in Italy. In the papacy of Clement VI Avignon's involvement with the war between England and France had been largely diplomatic and—it has to be said—largely ineffective. The pope's attempts at mediation had been received with the deepest suspicion on the part of the English on the grounds that his stance in the dispute over who was the rightful king of France was far from being impartial, which indeed it was. But now, under Pope Innocent, the relationship of Avignon to that conflict was to prove infinitely more serious and a great deal more calamitous. And it all began with a simple and fatal mistake on the part of the French—the continued refusal of their military leadership to learn their lesson about the deadliness of the English longbow.

In the autumn of 1356 Edward the Black Prince, son of the English king Edward III, was leading an army southwards from the River Loire with a numerically superior force led by the French king John II in hot pursuit. The two armies finally met on 19 September south of Poitiers; and here the French mounted knights repeated the folly they had committed at Crécy ten years earlier (and were to repeat once again at Agincourt fifty-nine years later) of riding headlong into a storm of arrows from the English longbowmen. Charge after charge met the same response, the final charge being led by the French king himself, who managed to escape with his life but found himself unceremoniously taken prisoner.

This catastrophic defeat for the French armies at Poitiers had dire repercussions for the whole country and—indirectly but disastrously—for Avignon as well. Having been captured, King John was taken the following spring to London where he concluded two treaties so disadvantageous to his own country that the defeated French immediately repudiated them. Finally in 1360 a more balanced agreement, the Treaty of Brétagny, was signed by both parties, and so began an uneasy truce which managed to last for nine years.

But truce brought the very opposite of peace. While the war continued the mercenary armies on both sides had been fully employed and for the most part fully paid. However, now that fighting had ceased for the time being those same mercenaries found themselves unemployed and unpaid. As a result a great many of them resorted to brigandage. Bands of them took to ravaging the French countryside, looting, setting fire to castles and villages, ransacking churches and monasteries, and murdering anyone who chose to stand in their way. Moreover they were far from being a disorganized rabble. They had been trained as an effective fighting force, and now they became an equally effective force of bandits, well-equipped and well-led. One of the earliest armed groups in the immediate aftermath of Poitiers was led by a notorious "arch-priest" of the brigands by the name of Arnaud de Cervole. His family seem to have been impoverished minor nobility, and Arnaud had become a professional soldier to seek his fortune. He had fought against the Black Prince, had been wounded and captured by the English, was released after the truce, then turned his talents to assembling a highly effective private army which proceeded to cut a swathe of destruction through southern France, heading inexorably for the most tempting city in the whole region—Avignon.

Here were some of the richest pickings to be found anywhere in Europe. For all Innocent's efforts at reducing some of the city's more conspicuous opulence, Avignon was still home to exceedingly wealthy cardinals and other members of the papal court, as well as to a large community of prosperous businessmen and bankers. The papal treasury might be perilously low, yet the place as a whole bulged with money. And men like Arnaud de Cervole knew it.

So, barely seven months after the battle of Poitiers the papal city found itself under attack. What was more, Avignon's protective ramparts, which had been torn down on the orders of the French king early the previous century, had never been adequately restored, and in any case the city had by now expanded far beyond those original walls. A new outer ring of defences (the site of the present-day ramparts), was hastily thrown up, but it was entirely insufficient, and Pope Innocent found himself forced to negotiate with the invaders in order to save his city from destruction. In the somewhat quaint manner of the times he invited Arnaud de Cervole to dinner in the papal palace, feudal rank being capable of bringing noblemen together even in extreme circumstances. Sadly no record of their conversation survives, except that we know discussions were concluded with the pope's commitment to pay Arnaud the huge sum of 40,000 crowns (which he was compelled to borrow) before the rebel leader would agree to withdraw his army.

The disastrous episode of Arnaud de Cervole and his band of mercenaries was only the beginning. The Treaty of Brétagny, signed between England and France in May 1360, led to the most destructive period France had experienced since the Norman and barbarian invasions of the ninth and tenth centuries. Outside the major cities there was no effective law and order of any kind. By this time a great many of the now-unemployed mercenaries on both sides had become organized into what have become known as the Free Companies, or *Routiers*—"vagabonds" or "men of the road". Their numbers had increased hugely, swollen by a motley array of adventurers, many of them from Germany and the Low Countries who had never taken part in the Anglo-French battles but who were quick to recognize a golden opportunity for a life of profitable plunder as they ransacked the French countryside at will.

Many of their leaders came, just as Arnaud de Cervole had done, from the ranks of minor nobility, often younger sons with no inheritance and no lands. The unofficial war they now chose to fight was chiefly against their easiest victims who were the peasantry, the people who worked the land and were virtually defenceless. Townspeople were hardly any safer, except those urban communities wealthy enough and organized enough to support their own armed guards on the alert day and night. In general the marauding Free Companies encountered little effective resistance. Their military skills were well-rehearsed, and their prey for the most part comprised unarmed peasants. In particular they favoured the strategy of surprise—the dawn raid on a village, the sudden swoop on a farmstead. But in addition to the rewards of straightforward plunder they soon learned to enjoy other sources of revenue which could be obtained with far less effort. Protection money was a special favourite; easy pickings were to be had from merchants bringing precious goods from abroad, or by offering safe conduct to travellers who, should they be foolish enough to refuse, might find themselves travelling no further than the nearest ditch.

It was a vicious and anarchic world, all the more tragic for being spawned from nothing more honourable than a vainglorious tussle over the crown of France conducted by two contenders neither of whom enjoyed a particularly convincing claim to it. The greed of two noble families had managed to reduce an entire country to a place of bloodshed and fear.

It was in December 1360 that the threat once again descended on Avignon. A contingent of the Free Companies besieged the town of Pont-St.-Esprit, just twenty-five miles north of the papal city and a town of strategic importance on the Rhône. Its fortified bridge had been built in the previous century at much the same time as Avignon's Pont St.-Bénézet, and it was the only other river crossing south of Lyon. When the bridge fell to the insurgents on the last day of the year the rebel army was able to set up camp on the east bank, and prepare to bear down on Avignon itself.

The city's ramparts and surrounding moat, hastily thrown up and excavated after the siege by de Cervole's militia barely three years earlier, were still far from complete. In fact it was to take a further ten years to finish the two-and-a-half-mile circumference of the new fortifications. In the gaps where stone had yet to be delivered wooden barricades and gates were hurriedly set up. Pope Innocent himself paid for armed sentinels to patrol the Rocher des Doms, high above the river, in order to keep watch on the approaches to the city from the north. Desperate pleas for military aid were rapidly answered from Languedoc and from as far away as Aragon, and such artillery as could be assembled was placed in strategic positions on the makeshift ramparts. And so, in a jittery state of semi-preparedness Avignon awaited the onslaught of the Free Companies.

The events of the next few months are documented only sketchily, if at all. Perhaps people had neither the time nor the energy to record what they witnessed during those winter months. Without question they were among the most agonizing times in the history of the city. As for the papal county, it fared no better. While holding Avignon under siege sections of the Companies systematically plundered the towns and villages of the Comtat, none of which possessed remotely adequate defences. For the inhabitants rapid measures of self-protection became a priority above all else. Of the larger communities Carpentras, capital of the Comtat (as it remains to this day), had its massive ramparts with thirty-two towers and four gates hurriedly begun at this period on the urgent orders of Pope Innocent, specifically as a protection against the marauding Companies.

The great fortifications of Carpentras were for the most part destroyed during the nineteenth century, though one of the gifts of aerial photography in our own day is to be able to detect, in Carpentras as well as a great many other communities in the Comtat, how the geometry of towns and villages in the region has been established by the shape of encircling ramparts and moats which were created for the most part during those chaotic days.

It is a dark irony that so much of the charm and character of the Comtat, and of Provence in general, as we enjoy it today, is the product of little more than a grim bid for self-preservation dating from the most horrific days of the region's history.

As it was mid-winter when the Companies plundered the Comtat, there was no opportunity to replenish food stores once these had been emptied by the raiders. Furthermore many of the most able-bodied villagers who would normally be tending livestock and working in the fields were now dead, killed defending their families and their possessions. Slaughter was widespread, and those who managed to survive faced starvation. Many of the country people tried to seek refuge in Avignon itself, only to get no further than the cordon of soldiers sealing off the city from the outside world. Those who did manage to make their way within its walls found nothing but famine and sickness.

As if to deliver the city a final blow, in the early months of that terrible year the plague returned. It was recorded that in the early months of 1361 17,000 people died in Avignon and the surrounding area, including nine cardinals. It must have seemed to those who had survived the Black Death only thirteen years before that the city was under a curse.

Faced with the plague and the siege, Pope Innocent gave in. For the second time within a few years he undertook to pay off the insurgents in return for their departure from Avignon and the Comtat. The precise terms of the agreement are unclear. It is conceivable that Innocent, having been powerless to drive the Free Companies from papal territory by military force or by peaceful negotiation, decided that the best course open to him was to employ them. If this was the case, then it seems probable that a condition attached to the pope's offer of money was that the mercenaries would in future place their military talents in the service of the papacy by helping to regain control of the papal territories in Italy. We know that it was to Italy that the

Companies promptly departed. We know also that this was the very moment when Albornoz and his nephew were preparing to seize Bologna. It is known furthermore that Albornoz came to have several detachments of the Free Companies in his pay.

Putting these scraps of information together, it may well be that Innocent's bargain with the mercenaries not only saved Avignon from destruction; it may also have contributed significantly to the restoration of control over the papal territories in Italy, so preparing the way for an eventual return of the papacy to Rome. And if this was indeed what happened, then Innocent's bribe to the Free Companies must stand as among the shrewdest political moves made during the entire span of the Avignon papacy—and this by a man generally held to have been politically naïve.

Among the most awesome fortifications to survive in the whole of France: Avignon's ramparts in the late nineteenth century, before the surrounding moat was filled in.

II

A Brief Farewell

In the winter of 1362 the River Rhône froze, and the people of Avignon were able to cross over to France on the ice. Pope Innocent had died a few months earlier, in September, and now his successor faced the coldest possible start to his reign. The enormous stone fireplaces in the papal palace were kept burning day and night.

This time, after the usual deliberations and horse-trading, the cardinals opted for a man who was not one of their own, but was certainly well-known to them and well-thought-of. He was yet another lawyer; he had once taught law at Avignon, and at the time of his election as pope he was abbot of the celebrated Benedictine St.-Victor monastery in Marseille, barely fifty miles away. He was Guillaume de Grimoard, a nobleman and, like most of the Avignon popes, a man from the southern region of France. After legal studies he had become a Benedictine monk, and had since devoted much of his life to scholarship. He was widely acknowledged to be a good man, learned and deeply pious—a combination of personal qualities not always associated with the Avignon popes. He was the sixth of these, and he continued the tradition of being unlike any of his predecessors. So far the sequence of the first five Avignon popes could be described in simplistic terms as "puppet", "miser", "monk", "emperor" and "book-keeper". Now, with Guillaume de Grimoard, an appropriate epithet would be "saint". In fact he was the only Avignon pope to be canonized, though admittedly not until five hundred years after his death.

In October 1362, six weeks after Innocent died, Guillaume took the title Urban V, a name chosen—appropriately in view of his lifelong ambition—in honour of his namesake Urban II who had preached the first crusade almost three centuries earlier. Appropriate too was the fact that in Urban V's' pontificate the lingering dream of "liberating" the Holy Land was to flicker briefly and for the last time.

No Avignon pope was more widely respected than Urban. At the same time few of the cardinals who elected him can have had much sympathy for his style of living, least of all those survivors who could still remember the golden days of Clement VI when life at the papal court had been one long festival. The new pope's horror of all forms of luxury was such that for his coronation he forbade the traditional ceremonial procession through the streets of the city, along with the feasting and public celebrations which had always followed. He remained quietly throughout the day in the papal palace as though this was still the Benedictine monastery from which he had just emerged.

From that day onwards Urban continued to lead the life of a cloistered monk. He wore a simple black monastic habit in preference to sumptuous papal regalia. He fasted frequently, spent a great deal of time on his knees, and when he retired at night he would stretch out fully clothed on bare boards in a bedchamber made specially for him as a monk's cell built of plain wood. If these were attributes required of saintliness, then Urban undoubtedly deserved the canonization later bestowed on him. The bitter cold of that first winter in Avignon would have warmed his ascetic soul.

Yet there was a great deal more to Urban than the self-denying recluse. He was the most scholarly of the Avignon popes. His love of literature and learning was profound and generous; he is known to have supported up to fourteen hundred students entirely at his personal expense, and during his eight-year reign he was responsible for establishing a new university nearby at Orange and two others further afield at Cracow, in what is now Poland, and in Vienna. In the heart of Avignon itself, within five months of his election he had founded a college and monastery to be placed in the hands of the Benedictines of Cluny. The abbot of Cluny was the very same Cardinal Androin de la Roche who had made such a mess of replacing Albornoz temporarily as military commander in Italy six years before, and was clearly a man who should never have been allowed anywhere near a battlefield. In Avignon he proceeded to enlarge the property given him by Urban by acquiring a patchwork of neighbouring houses and gardens, so making it possible for one of the most handsome of Avignon's Gothic churches to be built in the decades following: this is the church of St.-Martial, a huge hunk of a building distinguished by a rank of enormous flying buttresses, and overlooking what is today among the largest and most delightful squares in the city, with café tables set out in the shade of huge evergreen magnolias.

Pope Urban would have approved of the gracious setting he had helped to provide because he was a man who took a special delight in the natural world. It was at his initiative that the garden of the papal palace was considerably enlarged, and he particularly loved to spend time strolling in it on summer evenings—as though it was a quiet monastery garden in which to meditate and reflect. The place remains one of Urban's most touching legacies. And close by what is still known as Pope Urban's Orchard lies on a lower slope just below the papal gardens on the eastern side of the palace.

A more dominant legacy of Pope Urban's—as much the signature of Avignon as its famous bridge—is the chain of ramparts which, as you gaze at them from the banks of the river, seem today to be holding the city together in a giant brace. And if you half-close your eyes, blanking out the car-parks which have replaced the moat and the numerous restorations which have taken place since the mid-nineteenth century, then you have a view of the city much as the last two Avignon popes would have known it. The ramparts, two and a half miles in circumference, had been begun under Urban's predecessor as an emergency protection against the marauding Companies. But they were brought virtually to completion during Urban's papacy, the pope having given the job of supervising the construction work to his brother Cardinal Anglic Grimoard, whom he also made a bishop (so demonstrating that even saints are not above nepotism). By the time the fortifications were completed only Paris among cities in France possessed larger encircling walls. And if Avignon's ramparts are impressive today they would have been doubly so in Pope Urban's day, studded as they were with no fewer than fifty-six watch-towers set at regular intervals along the wall, as well as twelve larger square towers each of which enclosed a massive metal-hinged gate protected by a portcullis and by a drawbridge that could be lowered across the surrounding moat.

These vast new ramparts came at a price, imposing yet another strain on the already-depleted papal treasury, though here the papacy was able to reap the benefit of the early legal training which all the Avignon popes had received. It was a training which made them highly efficient tax-collectors. When the fortifications were first begun Urban's predecessor, Pope Innocent, imposed a salt tax to pay for them, salt being among the most valuable commodities in the medieval world as well as a rich source of revenue for the church. His successor, faced with the even greater cost of the fortifications now that they were almost completed, imposed an equally remunerative tax on a commodity no less invaluable than salt—namely, wine. (It is hard to imagine Urban's predecessors, who had so lovingly planted and cultivated the vineyards of Châteauneuf-du-Pape, ever considering such a measure, however urgent the financial crisis might have been.)

These were special taxes imposed for special reasons. The primary source of papal income on a regular basis was a tax of a quite different kind, known as the *decimae*, or "tenth". This was a tax which applied to all ecclesiastical benefices, and consisted of a tenth of any income received from those benefices right across western Christendom being payable directly to the papal treasury. No wonder Avignon was widely regarded as being paved with gold, even at a time when expenditure on fortifications and military campaigns in Italy were actually milking the treasury dry. Pope Urban also displayed a surprisingly unsaintly aspect of his nature by claiming what came to be described as the "Right of Spoil", this being the right of the papacy to inherit on the death of an ecclesiastic any personal property which the man happened to have owned—a decidedly grasping measure which took advantage of the fact that priests being celibate, at least officially, could have no acknowledged heirs or offspring. Hence the papacy automatically became every churchman's legal heir, a fiscal sleight of hand which any finance minister of our own day could only dream of getting away with.

Pope Urban's love of monastic solitude in no way interfered with the role of Avignon as the social and political capital of the Christian world. In the case of most cities within Christendom foreign sovereigns were by and large content to send ambassadors or emissaries when they needed to communicate important matters of state. But with Avignon such was the prestige and glamour of the papal city that they tended to come in person. There was even a time, in the early months of Urban's papacy, when no fewer than three monarchs were resident in the city at the same time. One was the king of Cyprus, Peter of Lusignan. The second was Waldemar IV, king of Denmark. And the third was the king of France himself, John II, known as "the Good".

The French king, who had been captured by Edward the Black Prince at the battle of Poitiers and taken to London, only to be released on the assurance of a huge ransom, was now in Avignon to champion the cause of a new crusade against the Turks. Urban himself nurtured the same ambition, and on a deeply emotional occasion preached a sermon in Avignon cathedral in the presence of King John in which he pledged his commitment to the crusading cause. The French king responded in kind, swearing at the high altar that he would personally lead an army of 150,000 men to the Holy Land.

It was heady stuff. But it was the stuff of dreams. The practicalities of how such a force would be assembled, and who would pay for it, were not permitted to dampen the joy of the moment. And that moment was short-lived. For all Urban's efforts to secure peace in the Italian papal territories, and particularly between the papacy and Milan, there was never any likelihood that support for yet another large-scale military expedition to the eastern Mediterranean would be forthcoming. Furthermore, in April of the following year, 1364, the French king died. And his death was like an epitaph for the entire crusading enterprise. Instead of leading his promised army of 150,000 men to the Holy Land, John died a prisoner of the English once again. In the terms of his original release hostages had been accepted in his place until the huge ransom could be raised, one of those hostages being a son of the king himself. But the young prince proceeded to escape from his captors, and in a remarkable gesture of chivalry John voluntarily surrendered himself to the English as a matter of honour. And so in London he died, taking the crusading dream with him.

§

From the bare boards of his monk's cell within the papal palace Pope Urban was visited by a very different dream, one that seemed—at least to him—to have a far greater chance of being realized than that of yet another full-scale military assault on the armies of Islam in the Holy Land. It was a dream which had troubled the conscience of all his predecessors in Avignon at various times, only to be shrugged off as an impractical fantasy or else conveniently put on one side for future occupants of the papal throne to deal with. Urban was the first of the Avignon popes to take the dream seriously, and to be prepared to act on it. What haunted the pontiff's sleep was the absolute necessity as he saw it of returning the papacy to Rome. It was his primary and most urgent duty.

The first essential step towards fulfilling this ambition was to bring about peace in Italy, without which no return to Rome would be possible, and it very soon became clear that Urban was prepared to achieve some kind of peace at almost any cost. In the last two years of his predecessor's reign the papal armies under the inspired leadership of the Spanish Cardinal Albornoz had come close to achieving such a peace. Albornoz had succeeded in wresting the papal states from the feudal chieftains who for years had assumed control over them. Rome itself was in a state of ruinous decay but was at last relatively peaceful. Most of all, in the long-standing feud with the Visconti family, rulers of Milan, Albornoz had secured control of the strategic northern city of Bologna. On the other hand Bernabo Visconti was never a man to accepted defeat readily, and in the early months of Urban's papacy he continued to harass the region of Bologna. The pope urged him to hand over the castles he had provocatively seized, and when Bernabo refused, excommunicated him, forbidding anyone to provide him with "troops, grain, wine, victuals, cloth, wood, iron, arms, horses, ships, merchandise of any sort, or money."

The events that followed are confused and confusing. What remains clear is that Bernabo, a ruthless political animal like all the Visconti family, comprehensively outfoxed the pope, making small concessions that were sufficient to gain him papal absolution while in effect costing him next to nothing. Urban, desperate to buy peace, hastily signed a treaty with the Milanese ruler which Albornoz, looking on helplessly, regarded as entirely "shameful", and appears to have ignored it. Urban's response was to sack his general (just as his predecessor had done in similar circumstance), transferring him instead to the role of papal legate to the far-off kingdom of Naples, where his military skills were of no use whatsoever. To compound this act of his political folly Urban then appointed in Albornoz' place a man whose incompetence in every area of organization had already been amply demonstrated seven years earlier when Pope Innocent had given him the very same appointment. This was none other than the infamous abbot of Cluny, Cardinal Androin de la Roche.

It was far from unusual in the Middle Ages for churchmen to double up as soldiers. Cardinal Albornoz was a prime example, and many a pope and archbishop donned armour and wielded a sword in anger. What is mystifying is that both Urban and Innocent, his predecessor, appear to have assumed without question that to be a high-ranking churchman automatically qualified a man to become a successful soldier. In the case of Pope Urban, a saintly and unworldly monk, one can only believe that instinct led him to place his trust in a kindred spirit, entirely overlooking the proven unsuitability of his choice. The abbot of Cluny, after all, was one of the cardinals who had elected him, and—perhaps more importantly still—he was a fellow Benedictine monk.

All in all, given the political ineptitude of Urban and his predecessor it can seem a miracle that their armies in Italy managed in the end to achieve a degree of peace and order in the papal territories, to the extent that it became possible even to contemplate a return of the papacy to Rome. For this they had one man to thank: their much-maligned general, Albornoz. Following his second dismissal, chaos at the hands of Abbot de la Roche inevitably returned. Pope Urban at least responded with a gracious apology to Albornoz, summoning him from his formal duties in Naples to ease the hopeless abbot to one side and begin to restore order to the papal armies. Employing his huge prestige and long experience of Italian politics, he proceeded in a remarkably short time to create a league of Italian cities—Naples, Pisa, Siena, Arezzo and Cortona—to combat the rebel armies of the north. Militarily this was the general's finest hour. By 1366 the opponents of the papacy in the north had been defeated once and for all. Albornoz then led a papal army into Rome itself, taking charge of the city. The stage was now set.

§

In June of that same year, 1366, Pope Urban made an announcement to his cardinals, to the Holy Roman Emperor, to Bernabo Visconti in Milan, and to the king of France, that he was taking the papacy back to Rome.

The decision came as a shock to a large section of the papal court. The great majority of cardinals appointed by the six popes who had so far reigned in Avignon were French, as were the Avignon popes themselves, not to speak of the substantial army of advisers, experts in one field or another, secretaries, scribes, librarians, chaplains, notaries, administrators, traders, suppliers of goods of all kinds, indeed almost anyone who had been recruited during the past half-century to join the papal cavalcade. All their palaces, or more modest dwellings, were in Avignon (or else in Villeneuve across the river, or in the Comtat); so were the vineyards and orchards which they had come to own. Furthermore their language was either French or Provençal. In short, their lives were rooted there, and in many cases their livelihood too.

The last thing the majority of the papal entourage wanted was to be uprooted from their home and deposited in a foreign city whose reputation was for hostility, disorder and dislike of the French, and which by all accounts was by now a semi-wreck of a city. The comforts and security of Avignon seemed like the promised land from which they were being ejected. The argument that Rome was the city of St. Peter and St. Paul, and therefore the rightful spiritual home of Christendom, fell largely on deaf ears, as did—even more so—the argument that Rome was in a far better position geographically than Avignon to negotiate with the Eastern church in Constantinople and thereby bring about the long-hoped-for unification of the two churches. It is doubtful if many members of the papal entourage cared much about the fortunes of the Eastern church. French creature comforts counted for a great deal more.

Matters grew worse for a disgruntled papal court. The new French king, Charles V, instructed his general, the future scourge of the English Bertrand du Guesclin, to lead a contingent of the infamous Free Companies into Spain in order to attack the king of Castile, Pedro "the Cruel". In one of those bizarre episodes which characterize so many military excursions at this time du Guesclin, who had begun his own military career as a freebooter, decided to divert his mercenary force towards Avignon for the singular purpose of demanding money for the journey to Spain. His force of an estimated 30,000 pitched camp on the western bank of the Rhône at Villeneuve, and waited menacingly while Pope Urban pondered on du Guesclin's demand for the huge sum of 200,000 gold florins.

History has left us no insight into the general's mind, but there are grounds for believing that there must have been more to du Guesclin's belligerence than treating Avignon as easy pickings for a hungry army. A certain anti-papal vendetta seems likely. There had already been bitter conflict between the Free Companies and the papal city. Pope Urban had gone so far as to issue a decree listing the crimes supposedly committed by the mercenaries. These included the burning of harvests, stealing flocks and farm animals, slaughtering peasants in large numbers, terrorizing the rich in order to obtain ransom, butchering children in their cradles, raping nuns, violating young girls and turning noblewomen into serving-maids in their camps, compelling them to perform revolting tasks of an undisclosed nature.

Urban promptly excommunicated the mercenaries en masse. None the less he still gave in to du Guesclin's demand, and proceeded to raise the money in local taxes, finally sending the money to Villeneuve together with a bull of absolution signed with the Great Seal of the papacy.

More humiliation followed. Du Guesclin, learning that the money had come from the people of Avignon and not from the papal treasury, returned the cash, insisting that the citizens be reimbursed and a fresh sum be raised from the resources of the papal court alone. The cardinals and other members of the papal entourage were compelled to dig deep into their silken pockets. Only then did Bertrand du Guesclin agree to lead his contingent of Free Companies away from the papal city and over the Pyrenees into Spain. Added to the cost of Albornoz' campaigns in Italy, as well as the price of Avignon's new ramparts, du Guesclin's blood-money would ensure that on the eve of Urban's departure for Italy there would be precious little left in the treasury.

The departure from Avignon was a huge undertaking. It involved not only transporting the personnel and staff of the papal court along with their families and personal belongings, but a vast quantity of furniture, artefacts, archives, equipment, supplies of all kinds, as well as the extensive bureaucratic paraphernalia required in administering a large part of the entire Christian world—most of which was to be shifted with the greatest reluctance on the part of just about everyone in Avignon except the pope himself.

The departure date was finally fixed for 30 April the following year, 1367. The caravan duly set off, and almost three weeks later, on 19 May, the papal party embarked at Marseille. Having no galleys of his own, Urban had drawn upon the generosity of friendly maritime states. Vessels were supplied by Venice, Genoa and Pisa, by the Grand Master of the Knights Hospitallers in Rhodes, and by Queen Joanna of Naples, the monarch who had

sold Avignon to Pope Clement at the height of the Black Death
nineteen years earlier.

The pope insisted on taking his cardinals with him, however
reluctant they might be. Few of those privileged French noblemen
can have imagined, on the day they were awarded their cardinal's
hats, that they would be destined very soon to endure weeks of
seasickness on their way to a foreign city in which they had no
wish to live. The majority of the papal court, a veritable army of
personnel with its accompanying baggage, was required to take the
land route, a laboriously slow procession which hugged the coast
under the protection of a detachment of Knights Hospitallers—
a role to which they were ideally suited, having traditionally
performed the role of ensuring the safety of pilgrims visiting the
Holy Land.

While the core of the papal court was wallowing at sea, and
most of the remainder were wending their way towards Italy over
land, many of the chief papal administrators remained in Avignon
in order to prevent what could have been a disastrous hiatus in
the running of the papal empire, now a tightly centralized unit
as a result of a succession of lawyers having occupied the papal
throne. In consequence, before long western Christendom would
have two administrative centres, Rome and Avignon. Pope Urban,
before his departure, had taken the precaution of appointing a
deputy: the Patriarch of Jerusalem, Philip of Cabasole, was created
Governor of Avignon as well as Warden of the papal palace and
Rector of the Comtat. The appointment was a vital one, and for
once the pope seems to have made a sensible choice, because all
major financial transactions relating to the papacy still needed to
be made through Avignon, at least until the papal administration
could be fully established in Rome. Avignon was in any case far
better-placed geographically for such transactions, being an
international commercial centre with bankers and traders of all
descriptions long established there, unlike Rome which had yet

to recover from the anarchic and decrepit state into which it had slipped for most of the past century.

§

So Avignon entered a curious twilight period in its history. On a practical level it still operated as the hub of Christendom, though its authority now belonged elsewhere. It was like a throne without a ruler, the capital of an empire without an emperor.

Seventeen days after sailing from Marseille the papal fleet docked at the port of Corneto, where the pope was met by his faithful general, Albornoz. It must have been on the latter's advice that Urban declined to go to Rome straightaway. Albornoz would have informed him that the Lateran palace, the traditional home of the popes in Rome before the Vatican was extended, was now totally uninhabitable, and that there was nowhere in the city where the cardinals could be safely accommodated. Accordingly the pope accepted the invitation of Albornoz to remain for the summer months at his own headquarters in Viterbo, north of Rome, where he had built a fortress. And here Urban stayed until the autumn of that year, eventually reunited with the remainder of the papal court which had arrived over land.

By October work on the Vatican palace was advanced enough for the pope finally to be able to take up residence. And so, sixty-three years after Benedict XI and the papal court had fled the city in fear, the pope was back in Rome. On the 16th of the month, accompanied by two thousand armed soldiers, Urban entered the city. This part at least of his great dream had been realized.

If Avignon now seemed an unreal place, a ghost of a capital city, then so too did Rome. Much of it was in a pitiful state of decay, the result of endless fighting between rival warlords over the previous decade. Churches were semi-ruined, and many of the palaces gutted and uninhabited. It was anything but the

Eternal City. At the same time the return of the papacy bred an air of excitement and festivity. The Romans were delighted and relieved to have their pope back where he belonged. His return promised stability, and with it new prosperity. The city became charged with fresh energy, and work to restore the churches and public buildings began in earnest. Dignitaries from all over Christendom began to be welcomed by the pope just as they had been in former times. Early the following year, 1368, lavish feasts and festivities were laid on to welcome the king of Cyprus and in particular Queen Joanna of Naples. Urban even presented her with that masterpiece of the goldsmith's art, the Golden Rose, traditionally awarded to the most distinguished visitor to the papal court. Later in the same year he received the Holy Roman Emperor with appropriate pomp and solemnity at St. Peter's.

Then in the autumn of 1369 Urban welcomed a high dignitary whose arrival in Rome seemed likely to fulfil another of the pope's most dearly cherished ambitions. This was the Emperor of Constantinople, John Palaeologus, The emperor proceeded not only to renounce the schism between the Eastern and Western churches, but publicly announced his submission to the authority of the pope, thereby opening the way to a unification of the two churches under the supreme spiritual authority of the pope.

It felt like a moment of triumph for Urban, a resounding justification of his idealism and his courage in bringing the papacy back to Rome, at considerable physical risk and in the face of powerful opposition from the majority of his own cardinals as well as from the king of France. This could have been—perhaps should have been—one of the golden moments in the history of Christendom. And yet it was not to be.

The sky was darkening. The pacification of the papal territories which Albornoz had so resolutely brought about began to look fragile. Albornoz himself was dead; he had lived only a few months after the pope's arrival. Without his iron grip on Italy old inter-city enmities were beginning to erupt again. The authorities in Perugia went so far as to hire mercenaries to threaten the papal city of Viterbo at a time when the pope himself was staying there. The commander of the mercenaries was an Englishman, Sir John Hawkwood, a notorious adventurer who had fought the French in the battles of both Crécy and Poitiers, and who had since become the most successful leader of the Free Companies in Italy, fighting for whoever rewarded him best, his most frequent paymaster being the city of Florence. Hawkwood's military achievements were already legendary throughout the Italian peninsula; he had evolved a way of moving soldiers from place to place with unprecedented speed by insisting they wear only the lightest of clothing and equipment, and by teaching them how to employ the English longbow whose deadly effectiveness he had personally witnessed at Crécy and Poitiers.

In the midst of a triumphal papal return to Italy, here was a formidable enemy for the papal armies to have to face. And suddenly the precariousness of Urban's position was looking alarmingly similar to that of his distant predecessors in the months before the papacy's retreat to France and Avignon sixty years before. Any siege and consequent pillage of Viterbo, a papal city with the pope himself in residence, would have precipitated a humiliating departure from Italy, probably for good. Furthermore, added to Hawkwood's immediate military threat was an ominous link with that traditional enemy of the papacy, the Visconti family, rulers of Milan, whom the Englishman was being lured to serve. In fact within a few years Hawkwood was to marry Bernabo Visconti's daughter, albeit an illegitimate one.

In this instance disaster for Pope Urban was averted. For reasons not entirely clear Hawkwood agreed to make peace with the general of the papal army, the man chosen to replace the late

Cardinal Albornoz, another cardinal by the name of Robert of Geneva. It seems more than likely that a considerable sum of papal money would have changed hands in order to secure the settlement. (The English mercenary certainly prospered mightily over the years. In addition to his prestigious Visconti marriage Hawkwood managed to acquire a sizeable estate near Florence, and towards the end of his life was appointed an honorary citizen of that city, a tribute celebrated in spectacular fashion half a century later in the form of a life-size equestrian monument of the great soldier painted in fresco on the wall of Florence cathedral by the hand of no less a master than Paolo Uccello, and which survives to this day.)

Then in November of the same year, 1369, an event took place which comprehensively destroyed Urban's dreams and plans. King Charles V of France, an altogether more resolute figure than his father John the Good, declared the annexation of Aquitaine, which had been a possession of the English crown for more than two centuries. The English response was predictable and violent; two expeditions landed in northern France and proceeded to devastate the countryside. The second stage of the Hundred Years War had begun.

It was a painful blow for Urban. Barely a month had passed since he had feted the emperor of Constantinople in Rome, with all the attendant hopes of a reunification at last of the Eastern and Western churches. Those bright hopes were now dashed. The agreement reached between the two church leaders in Rome had been conditional. The emperor had certainly not declared his subservience to the pope out of humble piety. Rather, it was something approaching despair; his offer was the price he was prepared to pay in return for military support against the Turks and their ever-growing threat to Byzantium. This was why he had agreed to travel to Rome, and why he had offered his submission to the authority of the pope. Now, in response, it was up to Urban to act.

For his part Urban knew well enough, just as his predecessors had known, that any military campaign to defend the Eastern church could only be possible with the joint cooperation of England and France. And now, at a stroke, any possibility of that cooperation had been removed, and with it any chance of fulfilling the pope's most cherished ambition, the unity of the Eastern and Western churches—unless peace could somehow be restored.

It was a desperate moment. The only course of action open to the pope, as he saw it, was to attempt to negotiate a fresh settlement between the two nations as urgently as possible. And any such negotiations, he felt convinced, could only be conducted if the papacy were close to both protagonists. Rome was simply too far away. And so, on that slender thread of hope hung the decision to abandon Rome once more and return the papacy to Avignon. From here, Urban declared, he would be ready "to work with all my strength" to end the war between England and France.

Accordingly, on 4 September the following year, 1370, Pope Urban set sail from Corneto, the port which had welcomed him to Italy with such joyful expectation almost three years earlier. The papal flotilla transporting the cardinals and the majority of the papal court consisted of thirty-four galleys, supplied by the kings of France and Aragon, by Queen Joanna of Naples once again, as well as by the people of Avignon and the Comtat—no doubt in relief and gratitude that their lord and paymaster had finally seen sense and decided to come home.

Disappointment in Italy was widespread, especially among the people of Rome, who now felt betrayed a second time. Another man who felt betrayed was that enemy of the Avignon papacy, Petrarch. His peripatetic life had taken him from Milan, as a guest of the Visconti family, to Padua fleeing yet another outbreak of the plague (which claimed the life of his son), then to Venice for six years before returning to Padua. At the time of Urban's departure from Italy Petrarch had moved with his daughter and her family into a house he built for his old age in the village of Arqua, a short distance from Padua. Here he received the news, and reacted with characteristic spleen and hyperbole: "Before my wounds were bound up or the balm had touched them, you left me!" The one Avignon pope of whom Petrarch had once voiced approval had turned out to be just as traitorous in his eyes as his five predecessors had been.

By the end of September Urban and the papal court were back within the walls of Avignon, rejoining the rest of the administration which had remained there all along. The ceremonies of welcome were reminiscent of the city's golden days under Clement VI. Already the hiatus in Italy seemed a mere aberration. Few people seriously believed the papacy would ever leave again: Avignon would from now onwards be the new Rome—for good.

Of Urban's own disappointment there is no record. Neither is there a record of his attempts to reopen negotiations between England and France. But then there would scarcely have been time. A little over two months after his return to Avignon, Pope Urban was dead.

One of the finest of the city's Gothic bell-towers built in the era of the Avignon papacy—formerly attached to an Augustinian convent in the rue Carreterie.

12

The Return to Rome

With a population of around 30,000 Avignon was now larger than any other French city except Paris (more than 100,000). Though not territorially part of the French kingdom Avignon had none the less become increasingly orientated towards France, largely as a result of a succession of French popes and the predominance of French cardinals whom those popes had appointed, together with a papal court which over the years had come to acquire a similarly Gallic bias. Avignon also enjoyed far closer links with the monarchy in Paris than with any other European ruling house. And with the growing number of French courtiers, noblemen and church dignitaries now owning property here, or in Villerneuve just across the river, Avignon had become a second Paris rather than a second Rome.

Religious institutions were also increasing in number, attracted to the city by the wealth of local patronage from successive popes and cardinals. The Carmelites, Augustinians and Cordeliers were three of the religious orders who created new monasteries within the newly-built walls of the city; one of the most handsome of Avignon's Gothic bell-towers, in the rue Carreterie, was erected during the years immediately following the return of the papacy from Rome, and is all that survives of the former Augustinian convent.

Avignon had also become a prosperous centre of international commerce and banking, as well as commanding widespread respect as a seat of learning. Many of the clergy who formed part of the papal court were themselves distinguished scholars, and their presence had the effect of attracting a constant influx of visiting intellectuals and teachers from all over Europe, contributing to making Avignon's university a vibrant institution. Its law school was as highly esteemed as any in France, reflecting the legal training which all the Avignon popes had received in their younger days. The sumptuous papal palace also now incorporated a theological college of some distinction, while the papal library had grown to contain more than two thousand manuscripts, among them rare Hebrew books, translations of Arabic works on mathematics and astronomy, and a wide representation of classical poetry and philosophy, as well as examples of contemporary writing in Latin inspired by classical literature, all of which was contributing to make Avignon one of the earliest centres of humanist studies in Europe, and hence a precursor of Renaissance humanism which was to flourish a century later, particularly in Florence. Ironically some of the most esteemed of these new Latin writings were copies of the essays and letters of a man who seldom had a good word to say about Avignon—namely Petrarch. But then the great man's literary reputation invariably neutralized the venom of his rhetoric—and it remains to the eternal credit of papal Avignon and its intellectual broadmindedness that it should have done so. All in all, Avignon in 1370 cannot have felt like a city about to lose its elevated status for ever. And yet within a few years it happened.

The final departure from Avignon was almost entirely due to the determination of one man. He was Pierre-Roger de Beaufort, from the same Limousin area of France as his uncle had come from, the uncle in question being the most outstanding of all the Avignon popes, Clement VI. Pierre-Roger was yet another lawyer and was qualified in both civil and canon law, which was unusual for a churchman at the time. He had been made a cardinal by his illustrious uncle at the age of nineteen. Now, on 30 December 1370, just a few weeks after the death of Urban V, his fellow cardinals elected him pope. He was thirty-nine years of age, the youngest of the seven Avignon popes and the last of them (at least the last of the official popes). He took the title Gregory XI.

Glowing epithets have clung to Gregory. He was described by contemporary commentators as being charming, cultured and scholarly. Others stressed that he possessed high intelligence, prudence, circumspection, piety, goodness, friendliness, uprightness of character, and a mind that was consistent in both word and deed. But they also added that he was severely dogged by ill-health.

From the outset Gregory found himself inheriting renewed strife in Italy. He was in an invidious position. His predecessor, Urban, had abandoned Rome for Avignon out of an urgent need to secure peace between England and France, without which no campaign to help the Eastern church was considered remotely possible. On the other hand no such campaign against the Turks could ever be launched or sustained without a platform of peace in Italy. These twin requirements proved entirely irreconcilable, because the moment Urban turned his back on Italy in order to deal with matters in France the papal states once again became torn apart by predatory warlords. He would have needed to be in two places at the same time. Given this impossible choice, Gregory chose Italy. He was convinced that the security of the papal states was paramount for the future of Christendom, and that they could only be satisfactorily governed from Rome. And this meant returning the papacy to the city where it belonged.

Unlike his French predecessors, Gregory was predisposed to like Italy. He felt at home there, and he spoke the language. He had been a cardinal in Rome throughout the three years the papacy had resided there under Pope Urban. Earlier, as a young Pierre-Roger de Beaufort, he had also spent a number of years studying in the papal city of Perugia where he had mixed with some of the leading humanist scholars of the day, an experience which left him with an enduring love of Latin and Greek literature (causing him later to be described as "the first humanist pope"). His respect for classical learning and the civilization of Ancient Rome would certainly have coloured his judgment about the virtues of the great city on the Tiber, thereby reinforcing his determination to return the seat of the church there—to the rock of St. Peter instead of the sentinel rock of far-off Avignon.

And so, on 9 May 1372, little more than a year after becoming pope, Gregory informed the cardinals that he intended "very shortly" to be leaving for Rome. It was under two years since his predecessor had abandoned Italy in favour of Avignon to the intense relief of most of his cardinals and much of the papal court. Not surprisingly the majority of the papal entourage were profoundly dismayed by the pope's latest announcement, and applied what pressure they could to dissuade him. They pointed out in no uncertain terms that the most urgent matter in hand was to try to bring about an end to the war between France and England, and that Rome was simply too far away for the pope to undertake the necessary negotiations. Gregory remained undeterred. In a letter to the king of England, Edward III, he wrote (using the royal plural): "Since we were first elevated to the supreme pontificate we have always had a heart-felt desire, which constantly remains with us, to visit the Holy City, chief seat of our authority, and there and in the surrounding countryside to set up our dwelling and that of our Apostolic Court." The Italian cardinals, now heavily outnumbered by their French counterparts, naturally shared the pope's viewpoint with enthusiasm, stressing the inalienable demands of Italy over those of France. One of them was Cardinal Orsini, who wrote: "I cannot foresee how peace can come to his domain if the pope does not reside in his own see... It is certain that if the king of France were ever to leave his kingdom and go to Greece, then his own realm would not be well governed."

The fates did their best to keep Gregory in Avignon. Both Edward III and the French king, Charles V, urged the pope to stay at least long enough to negotiate a lasting peace between the two nations. After the crushing English victories in the earlier years of the war the balance of power had shifted significantly following the appointment of the formidable Bertrand du Guesclin as Constable of France, since when the English had suffered a series of military defeats, and these had made them more inclined than before to be conciliatory. Gregory sent legate after legate to both monarchs to exploit this new air of compromise; finally after more than two years representatives of both sides agreed to attend a conference to be held in Bruges, as a result of which, in the wake of long and laboured talks, a truce was agreed for just one year.

As a result, two years after telling his cardinals of his intention to leave, Gregory finally felt able to announce to the kings of England, France, Aragon, Castile, Navarre and Portugal that his departure for Rome was now imminent.

But it was nothing of the kind. A year later another warning signal was sent out, this time in the form of a series of letters to neighbouring rulers requesting transport. One of these was to the ubiquitous Queen Joanna of Naples, who had helped transport Urban to Italy and back some years earlier, and now offered to put six galleys at the pope's disposal. Gregory's request was for the galleys to be sent to Marseille in September. Then without explanation the papal order was countermanded. And still nothing happened.

By now Avignon was in a permanent state of turmoil and indecision, with elaborate preparations for departure throughout the entire papal court forever being put into practice only to be put on hold, then re-started, postponed again, and then cancelled; and all the while ambassadors and legates from all over Europe were to-ing and fro-ing through the gates of the city bearing contradictory messages to their exasperated lords and masters. Faced with such widespread bewilderment and speculation, Pope

Gregory felt compelled to impose "perpetual silence on all men whatsoever" on the subject of the departure or non-departure, and on the reasons for these continual delays.

In fact the chief reason behind the pope's constant procrastination had little to do with the Anglo-French war, or with the recurring instability of the papal states in Italy. It was money. The Avignon papacy was effectively bankrupt. On top of the cost of interminable campaigns in Italy the removal of much of the entire papal court to Rome in 1367, then back again three years later, had proved to be crippling. Gregory was reduced to begging for loans. His allies loyally answered the call. The king of Navarre agreed to lend him 30,000 gold florins. The Duke of Anjou was even more generous: the sum offered was 60,000 florins, although the pope was required somewhat humiliatingly to offer his own jewellery as security.

It was not only in Avignon that the extended delays were causing disruption and discontent. It Italy the Florentines set about forming an anti-papal league among disaffected neighbouring powers to resist what they perceived to be a dangerous alliance of papal cities threatening them on two fronts—from Bologna to the north of Florence, and Perugia to the south. Then Bologna itself proclaimed its independence, and Gregory felt compelled to summon the man who had succeeded Albornoz as papal legate and military commander in Italy, Cardinal Robert of Geneva, to take command of a contingent of mercenaries in an attempt to recapture the city. In one of the most ignoble episodes in the history of the papal states the cardinal adopted a scorched-earth policy in an attempt to starve out the Bolognese, devastating the surrounding countryside and permitting the barbarous mercenaries to carry out an indiscriminate massacre of the peasant population. And when this policy proved fruitless, and Bologna held out, the cardinal let the mercenaries loose on the nearby town of Cesena, urging them on with cries of "Blood! Blood!" On 3 February 1377 more than four thousand corpses littered the streets and ditches of the town. A truce between the papal authorities and Bologna was eventually signed only after the pope had finally returned to Rome, by which time Florence too had sued for peace.

(The holocaust at Cesena and in the Bolognese countryside was by no means the last that Avignon was to hear of the infamous Cardinal Robert of Geneva, the "Butcher of Cesena". After the departure of the papacy to Rome he was to reappear in the darkening story of Avignon as the first of what became known as the "anti-popes", under the adopted title of Clement VII, whose fortunes and misfortunes will be treated in the chapter to follow.)

Historians have been divided on what finally drove Pope Gregory to make the long-promised departure to Rome. Some have baulked at the idea that his decision might have resulted from the blandishments of a woman; none the less there can be no denying that the arrival in Avignon of a steely self-assured lady from Italy did coincide with the ending of the pope's long procrastination. She was a young Dominican nun by the name of Caterina Benincasa, later to be canonized as St. Catherine of Siena and to become patron saint of Italy. She had already acquired a wide reputation for her rigorous asceticism and a fearless dedication to a variety of Christian causes, the most passionately-held being the necessity of mounting a new crusade against the Muslims in the Holy Land. And it was in order to champion this cause to the pope himself that she came to Avignon. The unlikelihood of any such crusade taking place at this time entirely failed to deter her from calling on Gregory to return the papacy to Rome where it historically belonged, as well as to help bring about peace in that land. She wrote to him to that effect with fiery rhetoric: "Forward! Finish what you have begun!... Vicar of Jesus, you must take your seat once more... Be the successor of St. Gregory... Come like a man who is courageous and without fear; and above all, take care, for the love of life itself, that you come not with a military

following, but bearing the cross in your hands, like the gentle Lamb of God."

It had been a woman, Queen Joanna of Naples, who had sold Avignon to Pope Clement twenty-nine years earlier. Now it was another woman— one who could scarcely have been more different from Joanna—who was instrumental in drawing Pope Gregory away from it.

Finally, on 12 September 1376, he boarded a waiting vessel docked under the lee to the great bridge of St.-Bénézet. Members of the Curia, the inner circle of the papal court and governing body of the church, followed him, and the fleet of vessels sailed downstream for a short distance before leaving the Rhône and steering eastwards along the River Durance, which formed the southern boundary of the papal Comtat. They passed the town of Noves, then the papal city of Cavaillon, and on as far as Orgon on the southern bank of the Durance. At this point the papal party disembarked and took the overland route southwards past Salon. It was hardly the happiest of departures: "Oh God," wrote a disgruntled French bishop. "If only the mountains would move and stop our journey." The reluctant party reached Marseille towards the end of the month, where the pope stayed for some days at the Benedictine monastery of St.-Victor until the galleys which Gregory had requested from Queen Joanna and other European rulers for so many years were finally assembled and prepared for departure.

On 2 October the pope stepped aboard, and the following day the papal fleet set sail for Italy. Eye-witnesses reported that Gregory was in tears, overcome by the knowledge that he was almost certainly leaving his native land for ever. In fact he almost left this world for ever; the fleet was caught in a ferocious storm which scattered the galleys and sank several of them. The pope's own galley narrowly escaped being shipwrecked. Eventually on 5 December the survivors limped into Corneto, the port a little north of Rome from which Gregory's predecessor had left Italy six years before. Then, after a period of recovery and stock-taking the reduced papal fleet continued down the Italian coast as far as the ancient Roman city of Ostia, and from there sailed up the River Tiber, arriving in Rome itself on 13 January 1377. For the citizens of Rome it was a moment of muted triumph. After all, it had all happened once before. Then gradually, with the pope now securely in the Vatican palace and relative peace reigning both in Rome itself and in the papal territories, it began to become clear that this time it might be for good. The papacy had come home.

Pope Gregory himself had only fourteen more months to live. Ill-health had dogged him for all the eight years of his pontificate, and it was said that in the end sheer exhaustion was what claimed his life. So the seventh and last of the Avignon popes died in Rome, in the Vatican, on 26 March 1378.

§

It was five months short of seventy years since Pope Clement V had announced that the new home of the papacy was to be Avignon. They had been seventy years of glory and disaster, equally mixed. Avignon had grown from scarcely more than a riverside village to become one of the major political and commercial capitals of the world, as well as the capital of western Christendom. The city had been at different times extravagantly wealthy and spectacularly decadent, the object of envy and revulsion in equal measure. But it had also been besieged by hostile armies, devastated by the plague more than once, plunged into costly and unwanted wars, widely vilified, even reduced to financial humiliation,

Now suddenly the great merry-go-round seemed to be over, and the citizens of Avignon found themselves occupying a city that had become something of a hollow shell. Except—on the surface everything seemed the same as before. Much of the administration of the papacy still remained in Avignon, along with the archives and the magnificent papal library, as well as the staff of librarians and secretaries responsible for their care. Finance too was still administered here, just as it had been during the three years of Pope Urban's sojourn in Italy. In fact, for the remaining year of Gregory's pontificate the Vatican continued to be financed from Avignon, money being ferried regularly, and sometimes perilously, by sea from Marseille. This meant that a whole phalanx of lawyers, bankers, financial administrators, book-keepers, scribes, secretaries, clerks, security guards staff of all kinds had to be maintained in the gaunt labyrinth of the papal palace just as though the pope were still in residence. The city itself, after all, remained a papal possession and had to be run as such, and the same was true of the papal county, the Comtat Venaissin. To this end a large body of administrators had been put in place before Gregory's departure in order to ensure that the government of both the city and the Comtat continued to operate smoothly. In addition a committee of cardinals had been left behind specifically to deal with attempts at mediation between England and France, however fruitless these might prove to be.

In other words the papacy may finally have departed for Rome; none the less it had left a long shadow behind it in Avignon. And as it transpired this was soon to prove to be a great deal more than a mere shadow. Those citizens who imagined, as they watched the papal vessel sail away downstream on that September morning, that they were witnessing the end of an era, and that a serene Provençal life now awaited them amid the splendid palaces and rich orchards and vineyards of the city's glorious past, were in for a rude jolt—because Avignon was soon to play an unexpected and radically different role in the story of the popes.

The last of the Avignon "anti-popes" following the return of the papacy to Rome: the Spanish cardinal, Pedro de Luna, who called himself Pope Benedict XIII, and held out against virtually everybody for nearly thirty years.

13

The Born-Again City

It was never going to be a smooth transition. The return to Rome signalled inevitable changes to the papacy that were far more radical than a mere move from one city to another. Not least of these changes was the strong probability that any new pope would have to be Italian. The stability of Rome itself, as well as the demands of its people, made such an appointment well-nigh inevitable. Such a decision would be far from universally welcomed; after seven successive Frenchmen had occupied the papal throne there were bound to be considerable opposition and resentment, particularly among the French cardinals, most of them already horrified at having to uproot their comfortable lives in Avignon and live among hostile people in a foreign land.

Not surprisingly there was a smell of rebellion in the air during the Roman spring of 1378. A nucleus of sixteen cardinals assembled on 7 April of that year in the hope of electing a new pope. Outside the walls of the Vatican the atmosphere was growing heated and menacing. Mounting pressure to elect an Italian was being exerted by the local nobility as well as by a bellicose Roman mob, all of which struck such fear in the hearts of the French cardinals that they became paralyzed into indecision, even though they still represented the voting majority in the College of Cardinals. They simply dared not vote for another Frenchmen, yet could not bring themselves to vote for one of the Italian cardinals in their midst. After days of agonizing inertia, and with the threat of violence from the Roman mob growing uglier by the hour, the French reluctantly agreed to look for a candidate outside the College altogether, and to leave it to the Italian cardinals to make the choice. By opting out the French managed to save their skins, if not their honour.

The outcome of this fiasco was the election of a sixty-year-old Neapolitan cleric named Bartolomeo Prignano, a man who had been papal chancellor to the previous pope, Gregory XI, and was now Archbishop of Bari. It is unclear why he was chosen in preference to other Italian churchmen; perhaps it was precisely because no one seemed to know much about him, though he was believed to be a devout man and a reasonably competent administrator—both useful attributes not always possessed by past leaders of the church. Accordingly on 18 April Bartolomeo was duly crowned Urban VI, and so became the first Italian to occupy the papal throne for three-quarters of a century.

Little did those Italian cardinals know when they elected him what an unholy storm they were about to raise. From the very outset Urban became transformed into a paranoid monster. His arbitrary and dictatorial behaviour rapidly alienated the majority of those Italian cardinals who had recently chosen him. As a result Urban soon turned on them, accusing them of plotting against him, which may or may not have been true. In the course of time, one by one they were seized and tortured—torture being one of Urban's favourite spectator sports. In the meantime all the French cardinals, as many as thirteen of them, had wisely left Rome for their own safety. A short while later they convened in the summer residence of the previous pope at Anagni, in the hills between Rome and Naples. And here on 9 August 1378, barely four months after the election of Urban, they issued a document declaring his election to be "null and void" on the grounds that it had not been "made freely, but under pressure." The papal throne was thereby pronounced to be "vacant".

Four months later, at the nearby castle of Fondi, and with the powerful support of the French king Charles V, the rebel cardinals elected their own new pope. He was Cardinal Robert of Geneva, a member of a princely family closely related to King Charles and a man we have already encountered. It was another major triumph for the French monarch: the papacy was once more an acolyte of France, or so it seemed. The new pontiff took the title of Clement VII.

There were now two popes. And so began the most serious split in the history of the Roman Catholic Church—known as the Great Schism. It was to last almost half a century.

It had been a symbolic meeting of the French cardinals at Anagni. Seventy-five years earlier the same place had been witness to a violent attack on a pope, Boniface VIII—an event which had precipitated the break with Rome and the eventual establishment of Avignon as the new papal city. Now it seemed that history was about to repeat itself. In that same Italian hill town the rejection by a body of French cardinals of another Italian pope, Urban VI, led to second upheaval within the church in which Avignon was once again to be the beneficiary—at least temporarily. It was hardly surprising that the pope whom those French cardinals decided to elect in place of the hated Urban should now choose to return the papacy to where it had resided for the previous seventy years. Hence, not long after having been abandoned by the popes, seemingly for ever, Avignon found itself suddenly the rival of Rome itself—the chosen capital of the "anti-popes". It was the born-again city.

§

The new occupant of the papal palace in Avignon following the break from the Vatican may seem to have been an unlikely candidate to occupy the papal throne, or even that of the anti-pope. Cardinal Robert of Geneva, as he was known before his elevation, had for several years been the successor to the great Albornoz as commander of the papal armies in Italy. Robert's military career had been characterized by a ruthless zeal which had led him, among other unsavoury exploits, to condone the devastation of the countryside around the anti-papal city of Bologna, and then to perpetrate the massacre of more than four thousand innocent citizens of the nearby town of Cesena. Yet the "Butcher of Cesena" was something of a paradox; this cousin of the French king was by all accounts a handsome, delightful and highly cultured young man (he was still only thirty-six), who was a liberal patron of the arts, and fluent in Latin, Italian and German in addition to his native French. It was said that he adopted the title of Clement out of respect for what he considered to be the most benign and generous of his Avignon forebears, Pope Clement VI, whose appetite for high living and an abundance of mistresses the new pontiff also appears to have shared.

Clement's arrival in Avignon was in fact delayed. Following his election by the rebel cardinals at Fondi the new anti-pope, being the military man that he was, had hoped to seize Rome and become the unchallenged *de facto* pope. But his military resources were far too limited, and local support for him in Rome was non-existent; in consequence he decided to retreat southwards to Naples where he was welcomed by Queen Joanna, forever a Francophile, only to find himself excommunicated by the very pope he had hoped to displace.

It was not a promising start to Clement's reign. Furthermore the people of Naples were a good deal less welcoming than their queen, and feeling increasingly threatened he left the city in May the following year, 1379, along with those elements of the papal court who had supported the rebel cardinals. Clement promptly set sail for the one city where he could feel entirely safe: Avignon. A month later the papal barge made its way up the Rhône to dock close to the Pont St.-Bénézet under the shadow of Avignon's great rock.

It was two years and nine months since Pope Gregory had said goodbye to the city from that same quay. History was indeed repeating itself. The very first of the Avignon popes, Clement

V, had owed his election chiefly to the influence of the king of France, whose puppet he remained. Now, three-quarters of a century later, another Clement had returned to Avignon, again largely through the influence of a French king.

Then, within a few months the king died. But as if to reinforce the ties of Avignon to the French monarchy, his son, the young Charles VI, paid a ceremonial visit to the city as the guest of Clement, staying at a palace which had been specially prepared for him across the Rhône in Villeneuve—a tactful piece of etiquette, Villeneuve being part of the kingdom of France. On the other hand when the two men dined together in the papal palace the chronicler Froissart recorded that they were served at separate tables, Clement's being placed just a little higher than that of the young king. The new pontiff might be the king's cousin, but unlike his earlier namesake he was not going to be a royal puppet.

The bond with France was to prove crucial to Avignon in one way above all, and that was finance. The split with the Vatican had inevitably deprived Clement of most of the church revenues which the Avignon papacy had previously enjoyed. Now most of those revenues were destined for Rome and the official pope, however unpopular he might be. Without handsome French subsidies the Avignon coffers would have been embarrassingly empty. Again it was Froissart who noted how overjoyed the French cardinals were at the young king's visit, since it clearly signalled the intention of the French rulers to finance the Avignon court. A few decades earlier it had been the other way round. Now without the king's support, Froissart wrote, "they would have been in but small estimation." In other words, they would have been broke. French royal support also meant that French church revenues would now come Avignon's way. In fact for the remainder of Clement's reign almost half the total income the city received came from France. Only when Aragon, ever the faithful ally, also declared in favour of Clement did substantial funds from outside France begin to swell the papal coffers.

Gradually the city began to regain some of its former lustre. The papal city was once more the scene of glittering ceremonies, lavish feasts and entertainments, as well as daring displays of horsemanship. These were held for the most part on the green island in mid-river connected by the great bridge to Avignon on the east side and to Villeneuve on the west; and it was here on Barthelasse Island that it is generally believed the youth of city would gather to dance on summer evenings "*sous* le pont d'Avignon" rather than "*sur*". And in the city itself, just as in the days of Clement VI, artists, scholars, men of letters and particularly musicians once more flocked to enjoy the patronage of the man whom a sizeable part of the Christian world chose to call "pope".

Nothing could have been further from the grim, paranoid world of Rome's Vatican under the crazed Pope Urban. Avignon now sparkled and soared. The years following Pope Gregory's departure to Rome had left the city rudderless. Building work had slowed almost to a halt. All incentive to expand and prosper had faded away. In the absence of the cardinals their *livrées* had become empty or were maintained by a skeleton staff. Now suddenly there was a fresh injection of energy. Work resumed on a number of the churches whose bristling white spires punctuated the city's skyline, just as they do to this day. Among the most handsome of the new ecclesiastical buildings begun at the time of Clement was the monolithic church of St.-Martial, designed to serve a new priory-college attached to the Cluniac monastery founded two decades earlier under Pope Urban V (and described in Chapter Eleven).

This renewed air of optimism seems to have arisen from a widespread belief, particularly in the papal court, that the grotesque behaviour and unpopularity of Pope Urban in Rome would inevitable lead to the cardinals choosing Clement to be his successor once the obscene Urban finally died, and that this in turn would bring to an end the schism within the church which was causing such bewilderment throughout Europe. In the cherished dreams of the French cardinals such an outcome would finally ensure that Avignon, rather than Rome, remained the capital of western Christendom, and that the papacy would remain forever French thereafter. But they were dreams which soon proved to be fantasies. When Urban finally died in 1389—ostensibly after a fall from his mule near Perugia, though quite possibly as a result of poison—the Italian cardinals in Rome took a quite different course from the one the French had hoped for. Ignoring the claims of Clement, they proceeded to elect one of their own. He was another Neapolitan, who took the title Boniface IX. Avignon was now condemned to remain the city of the anti-popes—though not without a fight.

Clement himself died in 1394, five years after the death of the pope he had hoped to replace. He was to be the last French occupant of the papal palace, and the last of the flamboyant, high-living Avignon pontiffs. Hearing of his death the French king Charles VI, who had so respectfully visited Clement in Avignon shortly after his election, described him as having been "the true shepherd of the church". It was a description which ignored the fact that the shepherd had also once been a mass-murderer.

§

Following Clement's death Avignon entered the most unreal period in its history. It was a prolonged dusk in which its citizens, as well as members of the papal court, became increasingly at odds with each other as they stumbled to find a road back into the world of authority and power which they had once ruled, but which had mysteriously moved away from them. The city was gradually becoming Avignon the Lost.

Twenty-one cardinals now met in the papal palace to elect Clement's successor, eleven of them being French. The man they voted for was—surprisingly—not a Frenchman but a Spanish nobleman from that staunch ally of Avignon, the kingdom of Aragon. On the other hand he maintained the tradition of the Avignon pontiffs in being a lawyer, one who had taught in France, having been professor of canon law at the University of Montpellier. He was Cardinal Pedro de Luna. A further link with the Avignon papacy was that it had been Pope Gregory who had appointed him a cardinal. His native language was also Catalan, which was not far removed from Provençal, the common language of the people of Avignon. So, although a foreigner he was far from being a stranger in his adopted city.

Cardinal de Luna took the title of Benedict XIII. He was to be the last of the Avignon popes (or anti-popes), and in some respects he was the most intriguing of them all. He was certainly the most implacably stubborn and the most tragic, destined as he was to bring the final curtain down on the Avignon papacy in a manner worthy of a stage melodrama.

At first the ambitions of the new anti-pope seem to have been practical and straightforward, and they make it clear why his election was widely received with enthusiasm. He had been a vociferous advocate of church unity, proclaiming his belief in what was known as the "Way of Cession". This was a proposed solution to the present schism which involved the abdication of both rival popes, Boniface in Rome as well as Benedict himself in Avignon. In this way one single pope could then be elected. It appeared the only possible way forward, and in February 1395, a few months after Benedict's election, King Charles VI of France showed his enthusiasm for the solution by summoning a large body of leading clerics to Paris in order to discuss and formulate the terms of such an agreement. Three months later, in May, an imposing flotilla of French dignitaries was to be seen sailing down the Rhône in the direction of Avignon. The party included the king's brother the Duke of Orleans and two of the royal uncles, the dukes of Berry and Burgundy, accompanied by an extensive and colourful retinue of attendants and hangers-on. The purpose of this royal mission was quite simply to urge Benedict to abdicate, which before his election he had made clear his willingness to do. A certain diplomatic caution was required; being now the Vicar of God Benedict could hardly be ordered, or even requested, to keep such a promise. It could only be politely suggested to him that this would be the best course. Hence the pomp and formality of the French king's approach, and such an imposing cargo of dignitaries.

The royal flotilla docked close to the Pont St.-Bénézet and the party was escorted into the city where Benedict duly received them in the papal palace. That evening he entertained them lavishly, and for a while all appears to have been sweetness and light, with an Avignon pope adopting the traditional role of playing generous host to representatives of his most loyal supporter, the French monarch.

But then came the time for talks between the pontiff and the royal ambassadors. Suddenly it became obvious that Benedict was no longer remotely in favour of the Way of Cession, and that he had no intention whatsoever of abdicating. "I would rather be buried alive," he is reported to have declared. The talks dissolved into stalemate.

From this moment events in Avignon began to grow darker. Frustrated in their attempts to win any agreement from Benedict, the royal ambassadors succeeded in winning the support of many of the leading local citizens of the city and the papal court. They played on the traditional alliance between the city and the French crown, and no doubt stressed that the pope was, after all, a foreigner. But the resulting isolation of Benedict only hardened the pontiff's stubbornness. Pressure on the pontiff became increasingly intense: even the French cardinals who had elected him began to voice their disillusionment. Meanwhile in Rome there could be no question of Boniface even considering abdicating while an "anti-pope" persisted in calling himself the true Vicar of God.

The stalemate dragged on for months, then years. Finally, in July 1398, three and a half years after the royal ambassadors had first implored Benedict to abdicate, the French king took the crucial step of withdrawing his obedience to the Avignon pope in favour of the pope in Rome. All but five of the cardinals followed suit, while a general assembly of French clergy denounced Benedict for "creating and fostering schism."

It spelt disaster for Benedict. Not only was he now virtually alone in the Christian world, but with French papal revenues now cut off he was all but penniless. The great Avignon palace, for so long the scene of feasting and festivity, a place given over to excess of every kind, a magnet for European rulers, churchmen, philosophers, artists, bankers, men of letters, men of commerce, men of science, had suddenly become a hollow shell. Most of the Curia and the papal court in general had departed. Benedict found himself shut away within those vast empty halls and corridors of what Froissart described as "the most beautiful and enormous house in the world", attended by just a few servants and a guard of loyal Catalan soldiers. Meanwhile outside the palace the hostile citizens of Avignon and the Comtat stoked their anger at their intransigent pontiff, jeering at him from beyond the walls and calling him "le Pape de la Lune", "the Pope of the Moon"—a derisory pun on his name, de Luna.

By September of that year, 1398, it must have looked as though Benedict had no choice but to give in. The French king and the cardinals were no longer content with withdrawing their obedience to Benedict; they wanted him out—by force if necessary. Between them they hired a villainous mercenary commander by the name of Geoffrey de Boucicault to attack the papal palace. Boucicault stationed his army in French territory across the river at Villeneuve, in the French king's own fortress of St.-André. The gates of Avignon were thrown open to his troops, food supplies and all access to the palace were cut off, and the siege began.

What followed was anything but the foregone conclusion Benedict's opponents must have imagined. Certain factors began to work in the beleaguered pontiff's favour. The papal palace had been built as a fortress in the first place, and now proved to be well-nigh impregnable, particularly since Benedict's nephew and shrewd military commander, Rodrigo de Luna, had taken the precaution of destroying all buildings that were within striking distance of the palace (so creating the open space known today as the Place du Palais). Then, though food supplies had been cut off, the tradition of entertaining on a huge scale meant that reserves of non-perishable or dried foodstuffs were vast; besides which there was a garden within the palace compound where fresh fruit and vegetables could be grown. The papal diet might not be exactly wholesome, but it was adequate, and could remain so for a long time. Lastly there was the character of the pontiff himself. A leading scholar on the Avignon papacy, Professor Yves Renouard, has described Benedict as a "physically brave and mulishly obstinate Spanish nobleman". Certainly he appears to have remained quite undaunted by his own predicament, even revelling in it, personally urging on his small garrison, forever devising fresh strategies to foil his attackers, and continuing to maintain that as the Vicar of God he was receiving God's help and hence inevitably would triumph over his enemies.

For more than a year Boucicault tried everything he knew. The assault began at the end of September with a bombardment by cannon. Since the walls of the palace were many feet thick the cannonballs did little more than chip away at the stone, though more serious damage was done by those that flew through windows or over the battlements, and Benedict himself was struck a glancing blow in the early days of the attack. Attempts to storm the palace proved no more successful, although at one stage a squad of sixty soldiers managed to penetrate the defences by crawling up a sewage conduit leading into the River Sorgues, a narrow tributary of the Rhône which runs through the centre of the city. Their unsavoury entry led them just below the vast palace kitchen, at which point they were detected by guards and hemmed in. Boucicault also tried tunnelling his way in, one of the tunnels being dug from inside the cathedral to the north of the palace. But these attempts also failed.

Then in November Boucicault was sacked. An air of resignation had settled on the scene of the siege, and perhaps significantly Boucicault's successor chosen by the cardinals was not a hard-bitted mercenary but a non-military figure, a senior official who held the title of Seneschal of Provence, and who straightaway established a truce, while retaining a blockade outside the now-scarred and battered walls. After nearly fifteen months Benedict was still effectively a prisoner in his own palace.

Two months later, in January 1399, news reached Avignon that a relief force was on its way from Benedict's native Spain. A small fleet of ships had sailed from the Spanish coast and had already made their way inland along the Rhône as far as Arles, a mere twenty-six miles downstream from Avignon. The cardinals responded nervously by fortifying the Pont St.-Bénézet and hastily dragging an iron chain across the river a little to the south of the city. In fact neither precaution proved to be necessary; the Spanish ships were able to sail no further than Tarascon fourteen miles away, the river being too shallow. And the following month, clearly having little appetite for a fight, the relief force sailed back to Spain, leaving the imprisoned pontiff as isolated as before, with the papal palace by now severely low in food and fuel in mid-winter, many of its occupants suffering from scurvy and struggling to keep warm by feeding the fires with roof-beams.

The siege lingered on through the whole of the next year, and the year following. Somehow the occupants of the palace managed to survive. Food and other supplies were smuggled in for the small garrison. One suspects that these breaches in security occurred because the mood in Avignon had gradually changed. The besieging troops, being lawless mercenaries, were deeply unpopular. Furthermore people were beginning to feel sorry for their imprisoned pope, admiring him, even if reluctantly, for his stubborn refusal to capitulate. Inside the palace Benedict himself vowed not to have his beard shaved until he gained his freedom.

One indication of how ineffective was the blockade of the palace came in the summer of 1402 when King Louis of Naples, a successor of Queen Joanna, the former owner of Avignon, found no apparent difficulty visiting Benedict, and even spent a night in the papal palace along with his retinue. We can only speculate about what may have taken place during that brief visit. It is as well to recall that the royal family of Naples were also the counts of Provence as well as the previous lords of Avignon itself. It seems more than likely that a plot of some sort was hatched between the king of Naples and the imprisoned Benedict because a few months later, in the following March, the seventy-five-year-old pontiff slipped out of the papal palace in the dead of night through a secret opening which had been made in the outer wall. Benedict was disguised as a Carthusian monk and was accompanied by a small group of men who included his doctor and a chamberlain. The escape had clearly been carefully planned because one of the city gates had been deliberately left open, and the party was able to make its way to a waiting boat moored by the Pont St.-Bénézet. From here they travelled down the Rhône for a short distance before heading upstream along the River Durance as far as the nearby castle of Châteaurenard where they were met by an armed guard which had been assembled by one of the Spanish cardinals who had remained loyal to Benedict throughout the long siege.

They were now safely within the County of Provence, in territory owned by the king of Naples, the monarch who had visited Benedict in Avignon those few months earlier.

Some time after dawn the following day, from the fortress of Châteaurenard high on its hill above the Durance the self-exiled pope would have looked back for the last time on the city which had once been the capital of Christendom, and to which he would never return. Today only two towers of that castle survive, yet with eyes half-closed against the city's modern sprawl the view of old Avignon just a few miles to the north remains much as Benedict would seen it on that last morning, with its great ramparts, its cathedral, its towers, its forest of church spires, its sentinel rock hunched high above the river, and of course its massive fortress of a palace which would never again be the residence of a pope.

§

It was the end of an era for Avignon, yet far from the end for the obstinate and unrelenting Benedict. He may have given up Avignon, but not his conviction that he was God's appointed representative on earth. Whatever the pressure there was never any question of his agreeing to abdicate. When the papal party reached Marseille it was Benedict's initial intention to set sail for Italy in order to assert his claim to be the acknowledged pope in Rome. Though such an endeavour proved quite impractical the goal of entering the Vatican in triumph remained his ultimate ambition. Meanwhile he was compelled to move from place to place, country to country, year after year, ageing far beyond the lifespan of most of his elderly followers, yet remaining active and resolved to fight to the end. He even enjoyed a few successes. Largely through the support of the French king's brother, the Duke of Orleans, he won back the allegiance of France, whereupon a number of cardinals rallied round him.

It proved to be a temporary reprieve. In June 1409, six years after Benedict's escape from Avignon, the two rival colleges of cardinals were brought together at the Council of Pisa, at which both popes were declared deposed, and a third, Alexander V, elected in their place. Not surprisingly Benedict refused to submit to the demands of the Council. And so the desperate wanderings continued—Languedoc, Roussillon, and finally his native Catalonia, all the time accompanied by a diminishing band of followers, and such possessions as he had somehow managed to extract from Avignon, including more than one thousand manuscripts taken from the papal library.

The final blow was delivered at a further council held in July 1417 at Constance. Here Benedict was once again declared deposed, and accused of heresy. His response was as defiant as ever: he excommunicated the entire council. But by now he had lost all international support (except, bizarrely, Scotland), and his last retreat was to the castle of Peñiscola on a remote headland in Catalonia. Here, at the age of ninety-four and all but alone, Benedict finally died. The precise date of his death is uncertain, either late in 1422 or early in 1423. What is unquestioned is that he remained unyielding and unrepentant to the very end, and it is claimed that he managed to create four new cardinals just two days before his death.

§

A macabre symmetry shapes the circumstances surrounding the death of the last of the Avignon popes, or in this instance the last of the "anti-popes". The castle where Benedict died had been built by the Knights Templar a century or more before the forcible suppression of the Order early in the fourteenth century. It had been the very first of the Avignon popes, Clement V, who had given his papal blessing to the hounding of the Templars and the resulting death of so many of them at the stake. Now, by the most bitter of ironies it was a hounded pope who had been compelled to seek a final refuge in a castle constructed by the very body of knights whom his predecessor had destroyed.

The Avignon papacy ended with a whimper. Yet as the City of the Popes it merits a more glowing epitaph. Its achievements were considerable, and the effect of them lasting. Many of those achievements were fairly invisible, even humdrum; they were to do with the structure and organization of the Catholic Church, the kind of institutional tidying-up to be expected of lawyers—which all the Avignon popes were. But there were other achievements that were altogether more splendid and certainly more spectacular. Avignon gave the papacy a period of relative stability which had been unknown in turbulent Rome. What that stability managed to bring about was a new papal authority and—just as significant— new papal wealth. The trappings of that wealth were sometimes decadent and corrupt, as Petrarch never tired of pointing out. At the same time the affluence of Avignon helped create an alliance of wealth and patronage which set the pattern for the glittering papal courts of Rome more than a century later, when the Vatican was to become a centre of European learning, and the popes themselves—those sacred monsters of the Italian Renaissance— became the proud patrons of Raphael, Titian and Michelangelo. The Avignon popes were their forerunners. And, like the Renaissance popes, they were often better at being princes than priests. When Pope Leo X announced on being elected early in the sixteenth century "God has given us the papacy: now let us enjoy it," he was echoing the sentiments of the greatest of the Avignon popes, Clement VI, who had exclaimed as he looked forward to a reign of regal self-indulgence, "My predecessors did not know how to be pope."

The legacy of Avignon today: the papal palace and medieval cathedral, now "embellished" with its nineteenth-century golden statue of the Virgin Mary, viewed from a nearby restaurant.

Postscript

After the Popes

Much of Avignon is still the city of the popes, at least superficially so. Conservation and restoration have played their parts well. The massive ramparts still girdle the old town. The medieval cathedral, Notre-Dame-des Doms, rises massively from its terrace beside the high rock, the only noticeable addition being an overblown statue of the Virgin which has crowned its squat tower since the mid-nineteenth century. The skyline of the city still bristles with Gothic church spires raised at the behest of popes and cardinals, or by the numerous religious orders which flourished here during those golden years. The city's most evocative landmark, the Pont St.-Bénézet, though shorn of most of its original twenty-two arches since they were swept away by the Rhône floodwaters in the seventeenth century, none the less still stands, having become a romantic rather than utilitarian structure now that it ends in mid-water instead of conveying kings and princes to the papal court from French territory across the river.

And of course there is the Palais des Papes itself, that labyrinthine fortress which has been home to no pope or anti-pope for more than seven hundred years, but is now the magnet for three-quarters of a million visitors each year, and since 1947 has been the beating heart of one of the most successful arts festivals in the world. It was in September of that year that Jean Vilar and his troupe of actors launched what was to become an annual event when they performed Shakespeare in the main courtyard of the papal palace.

The greatest change in the appearance of Avignon has been in its infrastructure. The city underwent a number of architectural evolutions after the departure of the popes. The Avignon we see as we walk the streets today is to a large extent the result of a move to recreate it as a classical French city during the mid-eighteenth century, followed a hundred years later by a radical opening-up of the overcrowded metropolis in the manner of Baron Haussmann's Paris, and which has given us the Place de l'Horloge and the city's principal artery, the Rue de la République.

After the papal return to Rome the city, along with the papal county (the Comtat Venaissin), continued to be owned and administered by the Vatican for a further four centuries. Authority lay in the hands of papal legates, and subsequently vice-legates. These were men drawn from the ranks of the cardinals, and they governed—with absolute power—in the name of the absent pope to whom they were invariably related. The habit of nepotism was rarely broken. The habit of prosperity in Avignon survived too, and in the early post-papal years the city continued to flourish. Italian banks did well, and so did a burgeoning textile industry. Before the commercial dominance of Lyon Avignon became the centre of the silk industry. Mulberry trees were planted widely throughout the region.

This continued wealth led to intensive building activity. Several of the monumental churches which had been begun under the popes were brought to completion towards the end of the fourteenth century, among them St.-Martial and the church of the Célestins. The handsome Gothic portal of St.-Agricol was completed towards the end of the century following, and shortly afterwards the flamboyant façade of the church of St.-Pierre, with its elegant twin portal divided by a central column surmounted by one of the most beautiful carvings in Avignon, representing the Virgin and Child.

The most striking architectural feature of that era immediately following the departure of the popes was the transformation of the Petit Palais. In 1474 a young Italian cardinal, Giuliano della Rovere, was appointed to the double role of bishop of Avignon and the city's papal legate. Since he was also granted five other bishoprics in France and three in Italy, as well as an abbey or two and numerous other church benefices, Giuliano was hardly short of money, and he proceeded to set about transforming the Petit Palais into an elegant residence in the style of an Italian Renaissance *palazzo*, constructing entirely new façades for the south and west of the building, giving it the appearance it retains today. As it transpired, this venture was only a modest overture in the cardinal's creative ambitions. Almost thirty years later, after a lengthy period of exile imposed by the Borgia family, Giuliano contrived to get himself elected to the papacy. And in a short time, as Pope Julius II, he assured himself a special place in the history of Europe. He drew up plans for the new St. Peter's in Rome. He engaged the services of Raphael to create a series of huge frescoes in the Vatican. And he commissioned Michelangelo to undertake what was to become the most famous sequence of paintings in the world, the ceiling of the Sistine Chapel. Avignon had been the place of apprenticeship for the most ambitious art patron of them all.

Curiously in view of Cardinal della Rovere's subsequent bitter feud with the Borgia family, one of the early guests at the refurbished Petit Palace, in 1498, was none other than Cesare Borgia himself. Thirty-five years later another guest was the French king, Francis I, patron of Leonardo da Vinci. The later history of the palace was somewhat less glamorous. When Avignon finally became part of France in the late eighteenth century the Petit Palais was unceremoniously sold. In 1826 it became a seminary, and in 1905 a school. Finally in 1976 it was awarded its due dignity by becoming a specialist museum of early-Italian painting, the two highlights of the collection being a dreamlike *Sacra Covversazione* by the Venetian artist Vittorio Carpaccio, and a small masterpiece by the Florentine painter Sandro Botticelli representing the Virgin and Child.

The Petit Palais was not the only palace to be created by the Italian rulers of Avignon during this period. The city's administrator during Cardinal della Rovere's period as papal legate was a wealthy banker from Florence by the name of Pierre (or Pietro) Baroncelli. During the last decades of the fifteenth century Signor Baroncelli built one of the finest of Avignon's Gothic mansions, the Palais du Roure. The most striking feature of his palace is its portal, which is surmounted by a carving in low-relief depicting the intertwining branches of a mulberry tree—a clear reference to the city's flourishing silk trade, which no doubt also helped fill the coffers of Baroncelli's bank.

In fact his family stayed on in Avignon. In the mid-nineteenth century the banker's distant relative, the Marquis de Baroncelli, opened the family palace to a group of young writers dedicated to the revival of Provençal culture and its traditional language known as Occitan. The group called themselves the Félibrige, their most prominent member being Frédéric Mistral, soon to become an iconic figure whose name has been given to streets and squares in just about every town and city in Provence. Mistral's services to the literature of his native south were recognized towards the end of his life by the award of the Nobel Prize for Literature in 1904 (or, strictly speaking, half the Nobel Prize, since it was shared that year).

Towards the end of the nineteenth century, the then marquis, Folco de Baroncelli-Javon, decided to abandon city life in Avignon in favour of an area of swamp and marsh to the south of the region where he devoted the rest of his long life to rescuing an endangered breed of local horses and breeding black bulls. He duly became the father-figure of that beautiful if mosquito-ridden area of the Rhône delta known as the Camargue, where the famous white horses he rescued are now part of the irresistible folklore of the place as they prance elegantly across the shallow lagoons against a background of bulls and scarlet flamingos.

Meanwhile the papal palace itself had long fallen into a state of decay. The lengthy siege imposed when the last of the anti-popes, Benedict XIII, stubbornly held out there, had left the building seriously damaged. After Benedict finally slipped out of Avignon by night in 1403 to begin his long nomadic exile, the palace continued to be held defiantly by his nephew Rodrigo de Luna with the aid of a few loyal Catalan supporters, managing to withstand two further sieges which caused further damage to the structure of the palace. In 1413 a severe fire broke out, destroying much of the kitchen area as well as several of Giovannetti's frescoes. Eventually the last vestiges of the anti-popes slipped away, and the authority of the Vatican became established, with the first of the new papal legates taking possession of the wrecked palace in the year 1433.

In fact the legates never lived there. After the departure of Cardinal della Rovere (who preferred to live in the Petit Palais, which he had substantially rebuilt) the subsequent legates were invariably absentees. The French legates preferred to live in Paris, or on their family domains, while the Italians who succeeded them from the end of the sixteenth century chose Rome—which, considering that they were usually the popes' nephews, was understandable enough. "Legate" became a mere title, a sinecure. As a result the post of vice-legate was created in order to provide the city with a governor who was actually in residence. So for the following two centuries an administration which was essentially Italian controlled both the city itself as well as the Comtat Venaissin. The entire area became in effect a colonial province of Rome, and Avignon itself *Altera Roma*.

There are many tales, and many legends, relating to the Italian administrators of the city and the papal Comtat during those long centuries before the entire region eventually became part of France in the wake of the French Revolution. The men in charge were for the most part Italian clergy, and they were far from popular. There was widespread resentment at what were seen to be exploitative foreigners. The Italians tended to behave more like conquerors than governors, throwing their weight about, oozing with corruption, extorting punitive taxes when it suited them, treating the peasantry with authoritarian contempt, and often with violence. Debauchery was widespread, especially in the villages, where local girls were often corralled as mistresses by the local lieutenants in country villas conveniently far from Avignon. It must have seemed all too appropriate at the time that the hill-town from which the Comtat Venaissin had taken its title, Venasque, owed its name to the existence of a Roman temple dedicated to Venus. All this was meted out in the name of religion, and with the blessing of the Vatican. If the Comtat remains to this day among the least religious areas in all France, then the behaviour of those Italian vice-legates and lieutenants of God over a period of several centuries may be held responsible. Priests in the former papal county today can seem like an endangered species.

The Italian administration of Avignon and the Comtat finally collapsed less than a year after the fall of the Bastille in Paris. On 17 June 1790 the municipal authorities in the city rebelled and dismissed the last papal vice-legate, proceeding to demand integration into France. And on 14 September the following year the city of Avignon, along with the Comtat Venaissin, became officially a part of France. Two years later Vaucluse became the 93rd *département* of France, with Avignon as its seat of local government—though a further four years was to elapse before the Vatican formerly relinquished its claims to both the city and the Comtat.

Darker days: a reminder that following the French Revolution and the final eviction of the papal vice-legates the papal palace became first a prison and subsequently a military barracks throughout the nineteenth century.

As for the papal palace itself, from the moment Vatican power was removed all manner of indignities were inflicted on it before it eventually became the major tourist attraction it is today. In the year which saw the last vice-legate expelled from Avignon, 1790, the palace was turned into a prison for anti-revolutionaries. Half a century later one illustrious visitor to be shown vivid reminders of those dark days was Charles Dickens, who arrived in Avignon in 1844 with his wife and five children on their way to Italy. He found the city itself "quaint and lively... very like one of the descriptions in the Arabian Nights," and the cathedral "a bare old church". But what really whetted the novelist's appetite was to be shown the dungeons and oubliettes in the papal palace where prisoners had been incarcerated following the French Revolution. "My blood ran cold," Dickens wrote, "as I looked down into the vaults, where those forgotten creatures... starved to death, and made the stones ring with their unavailing groans."

The palace had remained a prison for a further twenty years after the Revolution, until in 1810 the military occupied it instead. If the prisoners had wreaked damage on the stately rooms, then the soldiers did so even more, hacking away statues, fragments of fresco, floor tiles, and ornaments of all kinds. The palace continued to be used as a barracks throughout the remainder of the nineteenth century, though in 1860 the government's restorer of historic monuments, Viollet-le-Duc, drew up a plan for its restoration, having already carried out extensive restoration of the city's famous ramparts. But the restoration plans came to nothing. The palace was only returned to civic use in 1906, after which a programme of restoration was finally launched.

Since then work has continued to this day, finally bringing that great hulk of a fortress back to something approaching the opulence and grandeur it once enjoyed in the days when Avignon, spiritually at least, governed much of the Christian world.

Appendix

The Avignon Popes

Clement V (1305-1314)
John XXII (1316-1334)
Benedict XII (1334-1342)
Clement VI (1342-1352)
Innocent VI (1352-1362)
Urban V (1362-1370)
Gregory XI (1370-1378)

and Anti-Popes

Clement VII (1378-1394)
Benedict XIII (1394-1422/23)

Bibliography

Allmand, C. T., *The Hundred Years War* (Cambridge, 1988)

Baddeley, St. C., *Joanna of Naples* (London, 1893)

Barber, M., *The Trial of the Templars* (Cambridge, 1978)

—— *The New Knighthood: A History of the Order of the Temple* (Cambridge, 1994)

—— *The Cathars: Dualist Heretics in Languedoc in the High Middle Ages* (London, 2000)

Barraclough, G., *The Mediaeval Papacy* (London, 1968)

Benedictow, O. J., *The Black Death, 1348-1353* (Woodbridge, Suffolk, 2004)

Bernardo A. S., *Petrarch, Laura, and the Triumphs* (Albany, N.Y., 1974)

Bishop, M., *Petrarch and his World* (London, 1964)

Boccaccio, G., *The Decameron.* (Trans, Oxford, 1993)

Bridge, A., *The Crusades* (London, 1980)

Brion, M., *Provence* (London, 1956)

Burman, E., *The Inquisition: the Hammer of Heresy* (Wellingborough, 1984)

Campbell, A., *The Black Death and Men of Learning* (New York, 1931)

Cantor, N. F., *In the Wake of the Plague: the Black Death and the World it Made* (London, 2001)

Cohn, S. K., *The Cult of Remembrance and the Black Death* (London, 1992)

—— *The Black Death Transformed: Disease and Culture in Early Renaissance Europe* (London, 2002)

Collison-Morley, L., *Naples through the Centuries* (London, 1925)

Cosenza, E., *Francesco Petrarca and the Revolution of Cola di Rienzo* (Chicago, 1913)

Dante Alighieri, *The Divine Comedy* (trans. Oxford, 1996-2003)

Deaux, G., *The Black Death* (London, 1969)

Duffy, E., *Saints and Sinners: a History of the Popes* (New Haven, CT, 1997)

Eco, U., *The Name of the Rose* (London, 1983)

Evans, J., *Life in Mediaeval France* (London, 1969)

Favier, J., *Philippe le Bel* (Paris, 1978)

Fergusson, F., *Dante* (London, 1966)

Foster, K., *Petrarch, Poet and Humanist* (Edinburgh, c.1984)

Gagnière, S., *Le Palais des Papes d'Avignon* (Avignon, 1985)

Gail, M., *Avignon in Flower* (London, 1966)

———— *The Three Popes: an Account of the Great Schism* (London, 1972)

Girard, J., *Evocations du Vieil Avignon* (Paris, 1958)

Given, J. B., *Inquisition and Mediaeval Society* (London, 1997)

Gottfried, R. S., *The Black Death* (London, 1983)

Hallay, A., *Avignon et le Comtat Venaissin* (Paris, 1909)

Hamilton, B., *The Mediaeval Inquisition* (London, 1981)

Havely, N. R., *Dante and the Franciscans* (Cambridge, 2004)

Herlihy, D., *The Black Death and the Transformation of the West* (Cambridge, 1997)

Housley, N., *The Avignon Papacy and the Crusades* (Oxford, 1986)

Huizinga, J., *The Waning of the Middle Ages* (London, 1924)

Kelly, J. N. D., *The Oxford Dictionary of Popes* (Oxford, 1986)

Lambert, M., *Mediaeval Heresy: Popular Movements from Bogomil to Hus* (London, 1977)

———— *The Cathars* (Oxford, Blackwell, 1998)

Larner, J., *Italy in the Age of Dante and Petrarch* (London, 1980)

Le Roy Ladurie, E., *Montaillou: Cathars and Catholics in a French Village* (London, 1978)

———— *Love, Death and Money in the Pays d'Oc* (London, 1982)

Leff, G., *Heresy in the Later Middle Ages* (Manchester, 1967)

Léonard, E. G., *Histoire de Jeanne, reine de Naples, comtesse de Provence* (Paris, 1936)

Lewis, R. W., *Dante* (London, 2001)

Mann, N., *Petrarch* (Oxford, 1984)

Martindale, A., *Simone Martini* (Oxford, Phaidon, 1988)

Mayer, H. E., *The Crusades* (London, 1972)

Menache, S., *Clement V* (Cambridge, 1998)

Mollat, G., *The Popes at Avignon* (London, 1963)

Morgan, A., *Dante and the Mediaeval Other World* (Cambridge, 1990)

Mullins, E., *The Pilgrimage to Santiago* (Oxford, Signal, 2001)

—— *In Search of Cluny: God's Lost Empire* (Oxford, Signal, 2006)

Mundy, J. H., *Europe in the High Middle Ages* (London, 1973)

Neillands, R., *The Hundred Years War* (London, 1990)

Oldenbourg, Z., *The Crusades* (London, 1966)

O'Shea, S., *The Perfect Heresy* (London, 2000)

Paccagnini, G., *Simone Martini* (London, 1957)

Peters, E., *Heresy and Authority in Mediaeval Europe* (London, 1980)

—— *Torture* (Oxford, 1985)

Petrarch, F., *Petrarch at Vaucluse: Letters in Verse and Prose* (Chicago, c.1958)

—— *Selections from The Canzoniere and other Works* (Oxford, 1985)

Prawer, J., *The Latin Kingdom of Jerusalem* (London, 1973)

Read, P. P., *The Templars* (London, 1999)

Renouard, Y., *The Avignon Papacy* (London, 1970)

Richards, J., *Sex, Dissidence and Damnation: Minority Groups in the Middle Ages* (London, 1991)

Runciman, S., *A History of the Crusades, Vol 3: the Kingdom of Acre and the Later Crusades* (Cambridge, 1954)

Russell, F. H., *The Just War in the Middle Ages* (Cambridge, 1975)

Saunders, F. S., *Hawkwood, the Diabolical Englishman* (London, 2004)

Southern, R. W., *Western Society and the Church in the Middle Ages* (London, 1970)

Sumption, J., *The Albigensian Crusade* (London, 1978)

—— *The Hundred Years War* (London, 1990 & 1999)

Synan, E. A., *The Popes and the Jews in the Middle Ages* (London, 1965)

Turnbull, P., *Provence* (London, 1972)

Ullman, W., *The Growth of Papal Government in the Middle Ages* (London, 1970)

Vingtain, D., *Le Palais des Papes* (St.-Léger Vauban, 1998)

Weis, R. J. A., *The Yellow Cross: the Story of the Last Cathars, 1290-1329* (London, 2000)

Weiss, C., *Laure et Petrarch* (Paris, 1935)

Whitfield, J. H., *Petrarch and the Renaissance* (Oxford, 1943)

Wood, D., *Clement VI: the Pontificate and Ideas of an Avignon Pope* (Cambridge, 1989)

Ziegler, P., *The Black Death* (London, 1969)

Index